We Need to Talk

new & selected poems 1970-2016

by

michael castro

Cover art: Cbabi Bayoc, "The Man Who Looked into Coltrane's Horn"

Photograph of the poet by Adelia Parker

Published by Singing Bone Press

www.singingbonepress.com

Library of Congress Control Number 2017938566

ISBN 978-0-9334391-6-0

For love, for poets I've known,
and for my wife and best friend Adelia

THE LONG WINK

old man
baby —

looking out
looking in

--Michael Castro

WE NEED TO TALK: CONTENTS

from **RIPPLE (1970)**

BROWN RICE

i love

making
brown rice
in the big
old pot

it will
nourish
every
body

after all
it costs
next to
nothing

to serve

4

from **THE KOKOPILAU CYCLE (1975)**

Homage to the Hopi

"Music is the healing force of the universe."
Albert Ayler

I. IT IS GIVEN

First, they say,
was only the Creator,
Taiowa. Taiowa
& endless space.
No beginning, no end,
no time, no shape,
no life.
Taiowa
the endless, the infinite,
created the finite —
Sotuknang.
Conceived him in a thought.
& Sotuknang gathered
the stuff of space,
molded it into forms,
& sculpted nine universes
one for Taiowa,
one for Sotuknang,
& seven for the life to come.

Taiowa looked at the work & said:
It is good.
It is very good.

Sotuknang gathered
more stuff of space,
drew the hydrogen & the oxygen
into a dance,
as he juggled the planets
round their stars,
the stars

round their galaxies,
he poured forth the waters
over each of the nine universes.

& Taiowa looked at the work & said:
It is good.
It is very good.

Then Sotuknang gathered
the stuff of airs,
cycled it into great ordered forces
given movement round each universe.
The solar wind blew.

& Taiowa looked at the work & said:
It is good.
It is very good.

Then Sotuknang floated into the first universe,
Tokpela, the first world.
Out of its dark earth
he fashioned Spider Woman to be his helper.

Spider Woman looked up into the light.
She spread her many hands about her,
gathered some soil,
molded it with speed & care
into a pair
of human-like-twins.

The twins stirred in their new world.
They opened their eyes.
"Who are we?" they wondered.
"Why are we here?"

Spider Woman turned to the one on her right:
"You are Poquangahoya," she said.
"Your job is to keep the world together & in order
so that life might live.

Go throughout the earth & touch it all over
with your hands so that it will fully solidify."

Spider Woman turned to the one on her left:
"Your name is Palongahoya," she said.
"Your job is to keep the world together & in order
so that life might live.
Go all throughout the earth & give forth sound.
Some day you will be called Echo,
for all sound echoes the Creator."

Then Poquangahoya stomped throughout the earth
molding its form.
The higher reaches of its body he made
into great stone mountains.
The lower reaches of its body he made
firm yet pliable
so that all who returned to earth in death
might use it during life.

Then Palongahoya shimmered throughout the earth
pouring forth sound from his cavernous mouth.
All the vibratory centers
from pole to pole
resounded his call.
Earth trembled,
& universe quivered in tune.

The whole world became
an instrument of sound,
echoing praise to the Creator.

"This is your voice, Uncle!"
Sotuknang sang to Taiowa.
"Everything is tuned to your sound."

It is good, said Taiowa.
It is very good.

from GHOST HIWAYS & OTHER HOMES (1976)

THE VOICE

I come to you with a tiara of rosemary
& whiskers of sage, & eyes
bright with the light of the dead.
I come to you from the taverns
of a violet dawn,
where chairs & bottles stack up
like cards of the scar-faced gambler
never learned his lesson,
smoky hours round ethereal tables,
crushed glass, ashes, & bones of dice.
I come to you from the streets of quicksilver,
& the golden bell of the saxophone flume,
& seep thru your pores like music,
floating to the drum of your heartbeat.
I come with the scroll-like lips
of the flower bat, with cloven mind,
with loco-weed dripping from my teeth.
I come to peel your artichoke petal by petal,
to unhinge your watery door.
I am the cube in your crystal of passion,
one fleeting flame in the crackle of your fire,
the worm that crawled out of your apple.
I am ghostly as buffalo
ranging & changing your prairie depression,
the pasture of your past,
your belly caked with tears of blood

drinking dry the creek of your breasts;
laughing lightly
& moving mediteranean fingers
over your aura's oud.
I drift like the moon in the clouds
of your calendar,
covering you with a tide of stars.
I meditate a kalpa
on your mystery's mandala,
cross your silent desert like a sun,
a red lizard walking the wall of your sky,
flicking my tongue at your morning lotus.
I am that tune you are humming,
the coded role in your music box,
the genetic key to the door of life
we are opening together
I am coming
thru

from **LIZARD TALES**

Lizard leaning on my tongue
lashing out language.
Flaming thru my mouth
a fiery flick of words.

After the flood goes down
Kingfisher, Lizard, & Coyote
gather up the bones,
sit around Coyote's hogan
casting 'em like dice,
gamble up the future
with the bones of the past,

& then lay bored. . .

   "Maybe it's time
      to bring the people back. . ."

they sit up thinking.
Lizard is smiling.

   "Maybe
     they've
        learned. . ."

SOLO FLIGHT
for Arzinia Richardson

The bass player's solo says

> *open a new*
> *door*
> *open a new*
> *door*
> *open a new*
> *door*
> *open a new*
> *door*

long fingers
   walking through time
into larger
   & larger rooms
until there are
   no more walls
just open space
   & stillness
thumping

> *open a new*
> *door*
> *open a new*
> *door*

THE TRANSPLANT

I am a fugitive of the Big Apple.
Left it in my youth.
Began a quest for truth.
Left behind the stony babble
of its brazen, craven towers.
Emerged into a natural space
& forged the track of hours.

I am a fugitive of the Big Apple.
Saw the garden overgrown.
Saw my actions overblown.
Saw the brambles & the briars
out on Mad Ave blot the sun.
Whistled in the subway wind
& watched my sentence run.

I am a fugitive of the Big Apple.
Singing the Jerusalemic Blues.
Eating what I choose.
Left behind my Father, split Man
hattan, shed the sea.
Snaking with the river, inward.
Planted my own tree.

TWO HAIKU

NEW YORK CITY

traffic jamming at
    Columbus Circle — gray birds
        fly south in silence

AMERICANA

His rifle cracking
    at Times Square Arcade —
        the hatless soldier

DRY HOLLOW

A lowing cow somewhere in the valley.
Crawdaddies dart & dig,
shovel up evaporating clouds
beneath the clear surface.

I sit on Dry Hollow's bank,
eyeing the sun's glint off the pool,
legs lotused, breathing deep.

Primal hills, bearded with trees, peer down.
An occasional hawk lariats the empty sky.

I chant AUM, AUM, AUM,
breathing deep, holding the mmmm's.

As I inhale, invisibly,
a cow MOO's, as if in answer.

BLOOD RIVER

dividing the body
capillaries like raw nerve endings
extending beyond the heart
into dark forsaken places
forests of two-headed serpents
crocodiles wallowing in red mud
shoots of wild grass taller than man
Blood River
surging through time
through a land mass
like a spinal circuit
carrying, shells, pelts, & feathers
visible traces of energy
on a *kundalini* ship
Blood River of the sun
changeable with the moon
the beating tails of reptiles
stir juices under its tongue
the teeth of its gates
more precious than ivory
shinier than light itself
Blood River
eyeless, not sightless
the mouth never closes
completely on the sea

MEETING IN WALES

we tread cow paths
over strange & hilly farms
looking for keith & hope

wells. good friends
are hard to find.
instructions seem vague.

around a bend an old woman
appears to float thru streaked barn door.
silver hair, pale blue glow

in eye, she takes our hands
& leads us to the river,
the way.

face wizened as an almond,
watching us, clouds drifting,
waves, as we cross.

FLAMING LOG

Blue smoke
eaten by night.

Years
of growth.

Warmth
& light.

from CRACKS (1977)

CRACKS

Seen a million of 'em
          Walking   Dyckman down
to Harlem   counting cracks   Dutch treat
          sidewalk cracks   ruling fields
                    "second over
by that big crack"   slid into
               home crack
cracked leg   local quack
          let me scream all night   wore
cast eight weeks   it too cracked
          window cracks   door cracks   china
cracks   germany, russia   ice
cracks
          hull cracks   nuts   bat cracks
finally hit it   high note   voice cracks
          bullet cracks   skin cracks fire cracks
cracks
                    in clouds   cracked
magazine   zone   yr cracked Al
          gonkian   stone   red
seam crack
shaman chiselled   woman round it
          spine crack   cracks   shell
cracks   snakes ooze out of   schools
          full of 'em   desk cracks   board
cracks
wise cracks   Levin looks up
                    at his living room cracks
                    crevasses   ravines
till the ceiling thunders down   cracks
          heads   wired cracks   liberty
               bell cracks   Sam
          choking with plaster dust   pounding on door
Al? Al? you all right?   cracks
          something
                    pushing through   saxi

25

phone   frage   Fleck's
              heart   tectonic pressure
nuclear waste   cunt cracks
        under fur   cracks in time
              something pushing
                              boulder
        cracks
flagstaff

                        pine

IN ST. LOUIS HEAT

the heat
*   the men*
in blue

jeans
    on the black
corner
by the Chester
Pipe
    Shop

Lean #
all
afternoon

        against
    the caged
storefront

GASLIGHT SQUARE

gutted storefronts
crumbling movie theater
empty picture
frame wall trick-
ling brick rubble
into street
eerie
& dimly fluorescent
uninhabited
save for one
solitary
stocking-capped black man
bent over
in loose drab overcoat
staggering between parked cars
in the driving rain

AFTER THE RAIN

robins

      hopping

            looking

                  down for worms

           & up

      for other

robins

ST. LOUIS BLUES REVISITED

Blue is the blues of this town
Blue as the cold cop
Who killed Michael Brown
Blue is the blues of this town

Blue is the blues of this town
Blue heat street sign blue core flame
Gas blue blaze haze glazes a name
Blue is the blues of this town

Blue is the rainsong, like tears it comes
From blue whale clouds that rumble like drums
Blue is the blues of this town
Blue is the blues of this town

Blue is the whiskey that gnaws in the gut
Blue is the uniform makes a man strut
Blue is the lead in the gun chamber rut
Blue is the blues of this town

Blue is the ghetto, blue the stone rubble
Blue the dope powder, blue the hope bubble
Blue are the trains, the veins, the migraines
Blue is the blues of this town

Blue is the ballpark, blue all the museums
Blue the caged monkey
                who swings between screams
Blue is the Arch, & the gateway of dreams
Blue is the blues of this town

Blue is the hit-man, blue in a bottle
Blue is the street girl, blue her eye shadow
Blue is the beat of the street & the news
Blue is the blues of this town

Blue is the song, blue the bird songster
Language as long & as strong as a dinosaur
The trees' teeth are chattering — airplane chainsaw
Blue is the blues of this town

Blue is the smoke over rims of the stacks
Blue is the waterfront, blue both sides of tracks
Blue is the love that is eaten by cracks
Blue is the blues of this town

AXEMAN IN THE WOODS IN WINTER
for Julius Hemphill (1938-1995)

He swung his saxophone in the streets
& begged in red longjohns
He swung for his shadow on the wall
          for a mound of white powder
          for a dollar bill rolled in his nose
He swung up & down the street in his red longjohns
People looked some listened all moved on
He swung his axe in the dense subway
He swung it down by the riverbank
He swung it across the Brooklyn Bridge
He swung for the clouds
for the herds of horses they became
He swung for sad folks down in their cups
He swung for the little boy who listened
He swung in his red longjohns
He thot of swinging with a monkey & a cup
      but didn't want no monkey on his back
He thot of swinging for the President
        but didn't want to lay down that track
He swung his own thots & didn't want
He swung for truth, for pain, for the action
      in abstraction
He swung for the pure clear ring he imagined
He swung to shake the bones round in their fleshbag
to hear them grind together,
to cast them out like dice
He swung because it was something he did
Maybe he swung because nobody cared
He swung to feel himself, to find himself
      to heal himself, unwind himself
He swung every day under the sun
Because it was cold outside
      he wore red longjohns

RE ORIENTATION

I wandered through creamcheese mist
                 toward a tomato sunrise.
My kora, heart's harp, rustled an ouzo love song
from flaming fingers melting plastic sliver moon scimitar
into quivering cloud cotton, cat mustaches,
stomach strings floating in crystal sky ball.
I had adjusted the midnight ear to the wheel's sweat
& lowered the thunder dial that the mountain might
hear clear my tundra coo.
In my pack I carried a jug of river wine, ticking broccoli,
a pinecone meditation.
I shuffled like a streetsweeper through the tear's desert,
oozed through the worm oil in caterpillar drive
sucking a brick nipple, munching orange peppers, breathing
   peyote fire from my upholstered breath.
I blew blake laughter into the vagrant voidness, watched
the starry dipper lift the sun from its manroot push-up,
its eastern exercise on the morning's chin
which dripped spittle of ivy like monkey lime
or cat's eyes slanting down a sheer moon dune.
Alone at the foot of the mushroom landscape,
I watched the turtle waddle of the rising
circus orb, felt its warmth pour through my tobacco fur,
& listened to the slurping condensation,
   to the green singing
     of my insatiable hair.

THE OTHER SIDE
for Helen Adam

Have you been to the other side?
Will you climb with me?
The other side of the mountain high
is unmapped territory

> *O yes I'll climb I'll climb I'll climb*
> *I'll climb with you till the end of time*
> *O yes I'll climb I'll climb I'll climb*
> *I'll climb that mountain fair-o*
>
> *For I've been there been there been there*
> *O I've been there been there*
> *The snow is falling everywhere*
> *But I've been there been there*

She takes his hand into her own
The wind is howling fierce
So cold the cold osmoses bones
As her words ring in his ears

> *O yes I'll climb I'll climb I'll climb*
> *I'll climb with you till the end of time*
> *O yes I'll climb I'll climb I'll climb*
> *I'll climb that mountain fair-o*

She draws him 'neath her red coat warm
Its fur crawls on his skin
He soon forgets the howling storm
& hears her words again

> *O I've been there been there been there*
> *O I've been there been there*
> *The snow is falling everywhere*
> *But I've been there been there*

34

They climb & climb & climb & climb
The snow falls blurry white
He sees flakes dancing yet feels blind
He can't tell day from night

A flash of fear: 'Go back! Go back
You know not where you go!'
He turns around to trace their track
But all he sees is snow

> *O yes I'll climb I'll climb I'll climb*
> *I'll climb with you till the end of time*
> *O yes I'll climb I'll climb I'll climb*
> *I'll climb that mountain fair-o*

His legs grow leaden, fingers numb
Her fur freezes to his bones
He tries to speak, alas, he's dumb
His words come out as groans

Her hand so fastly round his own
Turns bony as a claw
It grips him tightly then lets go!
The wind begins to roar

Oh yes I'll climb I'll climb I'll climb
The snow is falling everywhere
I'll climb with you till the end of time
Oh I been there been there been there

The snow is swirling round & round
It spins him like a top
Around, around, around the ground
He cannot see or stop

A dancing red streak in the wood
Breaks through the relentless white
A furry tail as red as blood
His teeth flash out to bite

O I've been there been there been there
O I've been there been there
The snow is falling everywhere
But I've been there been there

An eagle soaring o'er the peak
Looks down where a timber-wolf wails
An ice-drop glistens on her beak
The wolf leaps after his own tail

O yes I'll climb I'll climb I'll climb
I'll climb with you till the end of time
O yes I'll climb I'll climb I'll climb
I'll climb that mountain fair-o

Have you been to the other side?
Will you climb with me?
The other side of the mountain high
Is unmapped territory

Unmapped territory

Unmapped territory

Unmapped territory

THE SEASONS

I am change
I am the seasons
I have my reasons

I'm white & empty
& green & brown
& yellow & red
& everything said

I am change
I am the seasons
I have my reasons

Cold & cool
& warm & hot
Alive & dead
Old skin is shed

I am change
I am the seasons
I have my reasons

One time for plowing
& one time for seeding
One time for reaping
& one time for sleeping

I am change
I am the seasons
I have my reasons

from **(US) (1991)**

BIG GAME POEM

This is a poem to kill all the loneliness in America
as it is a poem to kill my loneliness
for loneliness is an only one
a one alone & missing
something which in America is never known
& so one is alone
It is a poem to eat loneliness out of the stone
prune it out of the tree
worm it out of the fruit
weed it out of the garden
It is a poem to kill all the loneliness in the Free World
It's a poem for the highway flat as Kansas
for the rush hour traffic & the subway crush
for massage parlors & grain silos
gay bars movie stars crow caws
broken mirrors & locked doors
& 13th story corridors
It is a poem to kill all the loneliness in America
& to kill my loneliness too
(Being a Leo, I like the Grand Design)
Can't get loneliness out of my mind
America is lonely
It has a big headache
Husbands & wives cross in their lives
Lovers do not realize
   who they are
      & why they are
One
   love ceases being
      fun   & then
they are alone. . .
Leo paces the savannah . . .
There is rarely game in his range anymore
When there is, often he is not
Lonely lions (I almost said lovely)
are pitiful creatures

They have lost their pride
They will cry out in pain if provoked
But this is a big game poem
It aims to kill all the loneliness in America
& my loneliness too
It goes off half-cocked, roaring—
It's aiming right at you

CAR TOGRAPHY (US)

                                        we

            are he re we are

w her e we   are   he re

            we are   he   re   w her e

                are we are

    w he re we

        are   here

                                    ?

DEEP MIRROR
for Katherine Dunham

She digs an endless root, cuts, transplants
Sets herself up as a root doctor in a powerful swamp
Sets herself up all right, sets herself all upright
She digs an endless root this doc of dance

Holds a mirror up to each patient's breath she do
Holds a sea up to a setting sun *o yeah*
Walks that same path Damballa Wedo do each day o
Slides across the sky on that endless root *hey*

Root doctor dancing, the root twists & turns
Flames leap at the center, the heart weeps & yearns
A flaming swamp flower reaches up to the sky
& down into the earth where the living must die

She digs an endless root, cuts, transplants
In the powerful swamp where the two rivers meet
The cuttings take hold through the earth,
of the dance
Of the blue people waking & quaking their feet

Gatekeeper Legba, an old man in tatters
leans on his crutch in the dust of the path
He points with his pipe & its tiny fire
To a place you can't see but know matters

Root doctor dancing, the flames dancing too
The garden is growing where the people are blue
She holds up a mirror that's deep as a gun
She offers an ocean to a serpentine sun

Ghede sits dapper at the edge of a circle
His cigarette dangles, right leg's crossed over knee;
Behind his shades an underworld darkens
Look in his eye dancer, whose "i" do you see?

44

She digs an endless root, cuts, transplants
The dead are awakened by the din of the dance
Root doctor swaying, the *loa* arise
They shine in her eyes now, she seems in a trance

Erzulie is mounting a bucking *bon ange*
She rides now in terror, she rides now in grace
She rides over the sea to the mouth of the river
She leaves you behind & she smiles
through your face

Doc digs an endless root, cuts through & transplants
Sea flows through the rivers & sings in the swamps
Blue people buckle, Damballah still shines
& Shango speaks surely through the cracks in time

Root Doctor the patient, the patient revive
Root Doctor I didn't think that patient alive
The mirror is cloudy, spirit floats in a mist
The sun's in its bed now, the sea has been kissed

Root doctor *loa*, root doctor up right
Root doctor darkness & root doctor light
Endless root opens the gate of the night
Serpent sun memory speckled & bright

Holds a mirror up to each patient's breath she do
Holds a sea up to a setting sun *o yeah*
Walks the same path Damballah-Wedo do we do
Slides across the sky on that endless root *hey*

CHUMP CHANGE
for David Hines

Nick hunches into Europa Bar.
His sportcoat is shiny with soil
& his face's deep wrinkles match the coat's
dark creases. Once
well-known as a saxophone player
whose night beat covered this jazz & river city
tucking it in with flowing, anguished,
shimmering sheets;
in recent years we'd seen him rarely, & then only as
a ghost of his former self, hungry & roaming
the crumbling streets, spaced out & filthy
wrinkles like river-ruts
cut by a flood of electro-shock)))(((
waves scarring his beachy face, leaving it
a worn shell, a burnt-out case. Rumors
of drug problems, money problems, love
problems, a crack-up, breakdown, Bliss
(the mental ward), the work-house,
swirled round his name
like thin smoke of a smoldering butt.

Nick drags himself into Europa & focuses
on our cheery foursome, bubbling & laughing
beneath the blank TV; & in our midst he recognizes
cherubic David, a former musical chum
& now well-known
as the mellowest trumpeter in town.
Nick arches his St, Louis self, strides right up
&, for openers,
blows:

"Haven't eaten in two days. . .
Been sleeping in this sorry suit. . .
Spent last night in City Jail. . .
Got released this morning. Guess what? . .

46

Crossed Market Street & found this. . .
I should say this found me. . ."

He flashes from his inside pocket
a paperback book. It's a copy of *Vincent Van Gogh's
Journals,* with one of Van Gogh's
haunted self-portraits
printed in blazing red on the cover.
We look up from the image of those flames
to Nick's sad, sallow mug.

He looks David in the eye:
"Can you lend me ten dollars, Dave?
I'll pay you back next month."

David screws up his soft round face.
It's just dawning on him who this is before him,
supplicating in the silence.
"Nick," he muses. "Now wait a quick
minute, Nick. . . How

you gonna be able to meet such a heavy
commitment,
                    Nick,
seeing as we only see each other now
once every ten or fifteen years?"

Nick comes back,
building, developing his theme:
"Give me five dollars, man.
If I don't pay you back. . .
I'll give you my horn."

David winces, bows, shakes his head, smiles: "No,
don't give me your horn, brother."

"Can you lend me three dollars," Nick wheedles,
his voice rising. "Three dollars!
Come on David, man. We used to jam

together!"

David, trying to lighten the sound,
& playing to an audience, sighs,
"You drive a hard bargain, Nick."

Nick returns on time to the head:
"Come on, man. I haven't eaten."

David digs
    into his pocket, gathers
    a palm full of silver, says,
"OK, I'll give you some change.
Get you a bowl of soup or something."

Nick accepts the coins, caresses
them without expression.
Shifts their weight in his palm.
"Chump change. . ."
he murmurs,
softly, flatly.

David double takes, elaborates:
"Don't know
whether it's chump change or not,
but it'll get you something to eat."

Nick turns offstage, slipping
to some unheard beat toward the door.
Suddenly he whirls & shouts:
"YOU GOT ANY MORE MONEY!"
climaxing
his thematic erection.

David, softly, steadfastly:
"Got no more money
    to give away. . ."

They stare at one another,

locked in a long, sad, silent note.

Nick gathers himself again,
& says good-bye,
shaking his head &
naming each one of us
with incredible care & precision,
lingering, enunciating syllables:

"Good-bye Dreadhead. . .
"Good-bye Beard. . .
"Good-bye Short-stuff. . .
"Good-bye Axe-man. . .
"Good-bye. . . Good-bye. . ."
& fades. . .

David, ruefully:
"Bye, Nick.
Don't give away your horn now
for five dollars."

BLEW IT
for Woody Shaw

through the tobacco haze
& the clatter of cocktails
through the stench of spilled beer
& the lurching boilermakers
out of the darkness of the pit
where the vipers of the night entwine
he gave language to the black rose

Yeah, they said, he gave language
to the emptiness they shared
he gave them prayer & they said, *Yeah*

he screeched from the ache in his balls
intricate & instinctive as a spider
his belly blown lines spun a symmetry
spanning the void, flies buzzed quizically
round his notes on their way to the silent gods
& the chorus echoed *Yeah*
as he quenched their summer thirst

He was troubled, he was troubled
by their trouble, for he took it on
sucked it into the bell of his horn
into his gut where it gnawed & got reborn
made it part of his own storm
& he rained, he rained like a dark cloud
he reigned regal as a pharoah, clean as a queen
o he fluttered like a monarch, like Chuang Tzu,
like a caterpillar waking up & finding out
he can fly

& no one wondered why, they just let him die
they just said, *Yeah,* & let him die

for he gave language to the black rose

& down, down in the dankness where its root grows
the cyclopean train shrieked in the tunnel of the soul
a thousand toilets flushed
& the excrement of the city rushed
& gargled through the labyrinthine network
of subway pipes
a murderous *shakti* current injected the third rail eye
with a lobotomous blindness he straddled
sinking his feet in the low slow quicksand
They said *Yeah,* & lashed him to the tracks
O he had to hear that iron Siren's song

When it came hurtling & wailing out of the darkness
he had to sing along
had to embrace that Golgothan face
for it was late & he was headed home
He'd had too much to drink & he couldn't think
He just blew what he knew to be true
giving language to the black rose
raining all over it so it grows

& no one wondered why
they just said *Yeah,* & let him fly

FREEDOM RING
for Dr. Martin Luther King

Dr. King, Dr. King,
When did you hear freedom ring?

When the bloodhounds growled & wailed?
When sherrifs locked you up in jail?
When you sat up front in a bus?
When you overcame for us?

Dr. King, Dr. King,
When did you hear freedom ring?

When the tap clicked on your phone?
When you prayed at night alone?
When a child returned your smile?
When you walked the extra mile?

Dr. King, Dr. King,
When did you hear freedom ring?

With civil rights writ into law?
With klansmen pounding at the door?
When you won the Nobel Prize?
When you looked into deep dark eyes?

Dr. King, Dr. King,
When did you hear freeedom ring?

When you lunched with congressmen?
When you marched with garbage men?
When your dream lit up the night?
When your soul beamed in the light?

Dr. King, Dr. King,
When did you hear freedom ring?

When you climbed the mountain high?
When the bullet let you die?
When your spirit rose to speak?
When you turned the other cheek?

Dr. King, Dr. King,
When did you hear freedom ring?

*

 Freedom ring, O' freedom ring,
When will we hear freedom ring?

THEM

I am an endangered species
yet I am human
& I am free
living in eternity

but also from birth
on this planet earth
in the system
of Them

Them been here
since the beginning of fear
Them dragged me wailing from the womb
Them'll bury me silent in the tomb

Them granted curiosity
& planted a forbidden tree
Them's tricky, full of mystery
Them writes the book of history

Them is nameless, Them is free
Shameless as authority
Them's blameless in non-entity
The same whatever century

Them calls me woman, calls me man
Them tells me what I can't & can
Them calls me *nigger*, calls me *jew*
Them's neat as a nazi, twisted as a screw

Them etches furrows in my head
& drives me from my marriage bed
to walk the furrowed path Them paved
lonely, weary, to the grave

Them draws me close
then rends me apart
Them aches my head
& breaks my heart

Them tells me what
to think & buy
Them brings me down
Them gets me high

Them pits me against
my sister & brother
(not to mention
my earthen mother)

Them runs amok
Them calls for order
Them signs the deed
Them lines the border

Them is rich
so I stay poor
Them says 'love'
when Them means 'war'

Them is the enemy
of all mankind
Them hides somewhere
in my mind

Them smashes the atom
Drones & clones are here
Soon Them or Us
must disappear

COMING TOGETHER
for Adelia

Where the Mississippi & Missouri meet
I met you, princess of the Nile.
We smiled across the table of Kansas
with its gigantic bouquet of corn.
You drew me toward you like the sea
does a river like the sun a flower
like some vast black hole in space
pulsing with contained light;
you swallowed the white night, wrapped me
in your Afric cloak, filled a bowl
with herbal smoke & pulled long & deep
& I drew too the musky draft
long & deep like the Mississippi itself
long & deep winding down from the frozen north
to southern marshy climes.
The dark willows of the south enfolded us
the balconies of New Orleans
the tomb of its voodoo queen
Marie Leaveau we stood below
its white stone face, streaked with human blood
& graffiti'd with cryptic scratches left by feline souls;

& we drew again long & deep
swallowing the night of flaming crosses
robed & hooded riders
limp bodies swinging 'neath the shadows of trees
Negress & wandering Jew
we swallowed these sad histories
nazis, billyclubs, snarling dogs, inquisitioners,
massahs, priests & governors
whirling in the smoky Mississippi
enslavement in Egypt, America, the body
whirling & winding in the smoke up to the sky

white as the bones of the death camps

white as the tufts of cotton plants
white & whirling in the night

Your Moses came floating to you
on a raft of vegetation
buoyant with meditation
He saw himself reflected in your eye
A pharoanic sigh clouded overhead
The spirits of the dead clucked their tongues
Out of the jungle came a rumble of drums.
A dixieland trumpet cried over the river
crumbling levee walls inside our minds
letting it rush & wind
freely to the open sea
bearing you & me
& the burden of our history
bearing you & me
on the waves of sacred mystery

Children of the Sun
  Man & Woman –

  One

  (our exiles
masked by knowing smiles

CLOSING DOWN THE BARS
for George Barlow

"I thought this was a town you could
have some fun in."
Everywhere we go the bars close down.
"I thought San Francisco was an open city."
The quality of light, the twinkle in the eye of the bay
the kamikaze cocktails & the hills,
graffiti on the walls
all whispered that here was where the continent
went over the brink, that here
was a city built for bards.
Yet here we are, closing down the bars.
Not enough time for a guy to stare into his drink;
they're stacking tables on the chairs, waving &
shaking sorry heads though locked glass doors,
closing down the bars.
No time to return to that place where catty-cornered
ladies of the night (we finally decide)
really did give us
their eyes; no time to finish out that line
of questionable reason, savor that drink
down to the dregs, write out that poem
flashed & vanished in the warm glow.
They're closing down the bars, & leaving
us to roam the hungry streets, to look out
over City Lights, to try to find the car.

I think those Chinese poets had it right.
A jug of wine deeper than thirst,
some woods, a shack, a stable or a cave
where clocks & locks don't rule;
where a glance across a smoky room
won't stop your heart;
where a man can piss on his foot, get crazy
in his cups & stagger around shouting out
the shards of his broken brain to the moon;

58

where he can sing his off-key song
to pulsing stars,
discuss desire with the universe;
where all the doors are open, or don't exist,
& the only glassy things that will close
are his eyes
when he's so blind that death looks kind
                as a sunrise, & life
laughs with the crazy crowing cocks

IF NOT YOU, WHO?

You who are abandoned, you who have disappeared,
You who exist only in the resurrected photographs,
    in the statues of memory,
  the fluttering beats of lonely hearts,
You who have vanished into your own drab cells,
 the warehouses of clipboards, the pinstripe prisons,
You whose parting gestures are ironic, whose words
expand like projective verse,
You who are swallowed by a jungle,
declared irretrievable, missing in action,
done & gone,
You who are the final term
in the equation of emptiness
that longs for a proof,
You who are erased from the blackboard of space,
You who sit calmly between whirling electrons
who breakdown like a sugar cube in a cup of coffee
You who sparkle in a child's eye,
or droop in a teardrop

You who these words surround, close in on,
You who in absence are more than a presence,
You who are vacant, obscure, wary, weary,
who enact rituals in the morning
mirrors of imagination,
You who go about your life even in death,
   or your death oddly in life,
You who are lost who we cannot lose,
You who lose so we cannot win,
You who are despised, you who are idolized, you
who linger mysteriously in the air
with your inimitable music,
You who we cannot grasp,
you who come home to our embrace,
You who span the poem's breadth,

who breathe the poem's breath;
You who we don't know, yet know,
     with every inhalation & exhalation,
     we desire, yes, we write for you whose name is

THE MAN WHO LOOKED INTO COLTRANE'S HORN
(1997)

THE MAN WHO LOOKED INTO COLTRANE'S HORN

Me & my main man Mitch perched in the balcony
of the Village Theatre waiting for Trane & sweating
that summery May be June of — was it '67? —
I was almost
22 & anyway it was Trane's *last year*
in the flesh (if you can believe it)
the warm up act? — get this — Ornette!
& believe you me, he had blown
us away. He had this Swedish bass player, David
Izenson (a balding descendent of the harpist king),
a modest man with a beat
would always surprise you & delight with his light
touch, & when he stroked with his bow
you wanted to bow
before the otherworldly beauty,
the fertile sound-shape,
you wanted to bury your head in the cave
of that Venus of Venusdorf resonating
to his biblical embrace.
Right then I began a life-long love affair
with the fat fat fiddle & we wondered
how anyone could follow such a set
had set the stage, warmed us up to fever fervor,
tuned our sensory apparatus to frequencies so fine
you could see
ghosts of the Yiddish Theatre
this dusty cavern used to be
floating by the drab curtain — Menasha Skulnick,
dapper, bobbing to the *b-b-b-bum b-b-b-bum* beat,
the snake charming wail
of klezmer cafe reverie, & Molly Goldberg leaning
out the window
of *yenta* heaven, shifting her spotlit palm

from *oy vey*! mouth
to lotus ear, to forehead, shading sax-squinting eyes
as if peering down the tunnel of some lost subway
station of the cross-
eyed homeless goddess, searching for the Trane who
now was officially late-
late as only a ghost can know — no one
produced Yiddish plays anymore,
the language was dying,
but the jazz of language,
the funny language of jazz still lived
at the Village Theatre & the Trane
that we all came to catch,
& be borne away by, Trane was overdue.

Though the air had been conditioned to a degree,
it had not been cooled.
We were hot & damp in the dusty seats,
drifting, leaning
back to where we were — New York,
the Lower East Side, the Sixties
The mean streets leaned in, hairy with hippies,
skittish with speed freaks, pulsing
with poor Puerto Ricans — only the Village Theatre
& the well-fed cockroaches remained
from storied days of threadbare
immigrant memories. Trane would come. Trane
would take us away.
But who knew Trane himself
was dying? O sure, the sun,
Ra, was dying too. In time. But more
immediately...
Dying was Vietnam. Vietnam's
death consciousness
was everywhere.
Vietnam had our numbers & Mitch & I were going
anywhere but there — Canada, jail,

certifiably nuts1-Y, 4-F. CO, AWOL whatever
it took to avoid that cold drafty death-trip.
JFK was long gone. LBJ had saddled up
the fat bullet bombs.
Bobby, Martin, Malcolm —
their days were numbered too.
But Trane? Trane was like Bird. I mean
his notes were scribed in the air.
In the cosmos. & now
we sensed he was in the hall. You could hear the
shuffling backstage. & suddenly, without fanfare,
the curtain sidled open.

Dark forms crowded the shrouded stage.
We could make out Alice,
stomping chords on the baby grand,
& that must've been Jimmy
Garrison plucky at the bass,
 & they were flanked by an assemblage
of street-wise percussionists, congas, bongos,
traps, gongs, talking drums, bell-trees,
mbiras, dombeks, vibes, all emoting
a kind of cacaphonous swelling, a biomorphic mass
vibrating something like thunder
& bird thought shifting
to the sound they say a tornado makes up close
swirling over the hillside. The ensemble
built a kind of primordial chaos, something
from the nothingness they shared, that shared them,
taking away our breath, & restoring us
to a breathless awareness, an alert anticipation
of an electrical storm of violent renewal

& then Trane emerged from the wings like a god
blowing in full stride & he reached out
with a finger of sound to the assembled
host charging

the eye of their hurricanish brew with a gleam of
life's coherent
insistent yearning, & they & we were off,
flying — Trane was down to earth, business-like
in an unremarkable brown suit. His face was
serious & intense
& he was blowing something beyond
harmony & rhythm, melodic snatches
from riverbanks of memory,
from the silt of the soul, interspersed between cries,
moans & laughs, & another music which was as if
he had wired his brain for sound
& was playing the 90%
we supposedly don't use,
levels of consciousness finding form
& expression in the awesome moment, the world's
madnesses & wars
swallowed in his inspired breath
& spit out with all their raw & jagged edges
painful & explosive & expansive
horribly beautiful in the larger patterns.
There was a point — how far into the set I couldn't
say
for after the initial shamanic shock
we were with him,
beyond musical or chronological time
but a point in this newly created space was reached
when something strange
went down.
A man rose from his aisle seat like an island
rising from the sea, a long lanky baldheaded, blue
pea-coated black man rose, &
as if drawn by an invisible life-line
bounded over the sound waves
& leapt onto the floating stage
to stand & shimmer & smile mesmerically close
to the saxophonic source.
Trane took no notice,
immersed in his immense immanence,

& the man smilingly swayed as Coltrane played. . . *a few of my*
favorite things. . . booo-waah! eeyaah! . .
as Trane took us out
to those unchartered places
once again the man shook
electrically registering each shock
wave & then turned
& peered down into the depths
of Trane's horn for forever it seemed
& then he looked back out to the oceanic
audience beatific & believing like Big Foot
must have appeared
after he stared into the hat of the Ghost
Dance prophet & saw in that emptiness
the whole world!

Trane kept playing
& the man stayed up there swaying
& then suddenly Trane stopped,
nodded to Alice & let her lead
the percussive swells of the underlying soundsea, &
he turned
& threw his arm around the silent witness,
& walked him toward
the wings, whispering god
knows what in his ear. The man
clambered down the side-stage steps
& back to his seat on the aisle
& within moments Trane re-emerged
to make us gasp at his rumbling
train of thought, & then again
the man bounded & leaped aboard
& swayed & grimaced & smiled
& buried his head deep
into the golden Selmer flume so that we could see
the light
of spot gleaming off his bald brown dome

as Trane played implacably unperturbed
through the intrusion, literally played
through the head
of the magnetized initiate, undampened, unwound
galactic, genetic spirals of philosophic sound, played
from some invisible mountaintop
through all our heads the unfamiliar
familiar epic notes,
mapped journeys through this world & others
& brought us all home to

    A Love Supreme
    A Love Supreme
    A Love Supreme

    ◆

eventually
       the man left the stage
       shaking his ringing head,
eventually
       we all left the theatre
       to journey our own
       seedy East Village streets,
eventually
       even the ghosts left
       the Village Theatre
       to its incarnation as the Filmore East rock
       palace, & suddenly

Trane left the set,
left this plane & planet
whose pain & madness & beauty
       he'd exposed
to his *obeah* belly & breath — having spit
his medicinal music on us
through his healing horn & false-face lips,
       Trane left us one night

insights, lessons, sounds
ringing his bottomless bell through all our heads,
like a blue locomotive Trane left us
& kept on playing

through, beyond

all the wars
& all the love
in eternity
within us all

from **HUMAN RITES (2002)**

POETRY IS

motion
 poetry is
e-motion
 poetry is
he-motion
 poetry is
her-motion
 poetry is
hurt-motion
 poetry is
heart-motion

 poetry as
a notion
 poetry was
an ocean
 poetry is
come-motion

 poetry is

NAGASWARUM PLAYERS IN ALL SAINTS CHURCH
WITH OLIVER LAKE

The sound converges from all four sides
of the vast room
unearthly, earthy, raucus, jagged, round —
four nagaswarum players
in walking talking meditation,
gravitating toward a living center.
Alan Suits brought these
long black hardwood horns back with him
from India along with a supply of reeds; he blows
from the East, Jay Zelenka blows from the West,
Jim Marshall blows from the North, & I blow from
the South. It's the Universe City
Nagaswarum Orchestra. No one is ready for this —
not here in the 1973
Midwest. But we're ready,
heady with the overlapping drones, hearing
& feeling the music vibrate head to toe,
filling the space we inhabit — All Saints Church —
Father Kelly lets us practice here
Wednesday nights when no one's around, thinks
we're a rock band
he's keeping off the streets. O the soundscape we
create! nagaswarum,
ancient gatekeeper's horns,
inside the palace now, threatening
to tumble the walls. Interior Gabriels. We rock
all right & night. Solid
ancient rock consciousness.
Massive movement of sound, inevitable as lava flow.
Rick Safron tinkles little bells
like water spraying above our rolling surf.

The saxophonic wind wails
in the front door, billowing with it sweet
scents of gigantic flowers, herb teas & pollen.
Our noses wiggle,

ears perk. We are refreshed inside our breaths.
Oliver Lake has found his way to this suddenly
sacred rec-room of All Saints.
His saxophone harmonizes, melodizes with these
nasty nagaswarum.
The intelligent sound smiles,
having found its long lost relatives.
The Universe City night is intimate as eternity.
We instinctively reconfigure
as petals round Lake's flower,
as solar system, as karmic
wheel of life. We understand
whale song inside & out.
Lake's monkish bald spot shines
in the center of our shrinking expanding circle.
All the saints look down, smiling.
Father Kelly turns over somewhere in his bed.
Strange forms invade his dreams.
Outside, autumn leaves fall & skitter along
gray city streets.

No one is ready for this music.

IF YA WANNA RIDE IT GOTTA RIDE IT LIKE YA FIND IT

Trust the flow Joe
   you never know
   just where you'll go
   but you get there o-
   k here today
   as they *say*
   what?

Trust the flow Joe
   the juice'll rush
   the river gush
   & pause because
   it must
The laws
   the laws are in-
eluctable
   the shadow
   cannot be held
o no

Trust the flow Joe
   just try & meld
   yourself into the fabric
   of the whole
   not to say
   in any way
the soul
   but just the blend
   of tree & roots & earth
or
   on another plane
   the simultaneous birth
of breath
& death
   remains

unexplained

Trust the flow Joe
 whatever you did is done
 whatever you had is gone
 you'll never find
 what's left behind
 yet today's new sun is the same old one
 & the waves you've begun
keep moving on

Trust the flow Joe

POET'S RAP

Gather up & gather round
a poet's rap
is going down
ain't nothing new
the evening news
colorfully true
st. louis blues
aching thru
mythhistory
& snaking round
the mystery
& shaking apples
from your tree
to lift you from
your gravity

Poet's Rap
It's a killer
Poet's Rap
It's a killer

       Now
times are hard
careening fast
& each new day
could be our last
more reason to
use heads & hearts
& not abuse
our natural smarts
cause any answer
we can find
delving deep
in heart of mind

down in its depths
& still as stone
we understand
we're not alone

Poet's Rap
It's a thriller
Poet's Rap
It's a thriller

                    Yet
          in our time
we separate
& seeds get sown
of fear & hate
this rap reminds us
real-ize
              life's unity
that underlies
our lonely separate
transient me's
our individualities
              & know
compassion's
what we need
to full-fill life
not self-ish greed

Poet's Rap
it's a yearning
Poet's Rap
It's life-affirming

Beau Jesus says so
Buddha too
& Martin, Black Elk

& Lao Tzu
& every animal
through whose eyes
a soul cries out
we recognize
each still small voice
says, to be free
we must express
our unity
& bathe each self
in selfless bliss
as lovers do
inside a kiss

Poet's Rap
Thou art That
Poet's Rap
Thou art That

So
            expand that
I-dentity
& understand
"I'm" not just "me"
& that the inside
& the out
is what we're finally
        all
about
The universe is
where we are
eternity's
more near than far
the final Word is
All is One
So now you know

The rap's undone

Poet's Rap
It'll haunt ya
Poet's Rap
It's a mantra

       it's a mantra

            it's a mantra

BECOMING KRISHNA

Gopalakrishnan, the South Indian flutist, offstage
is unimpressive — a slight, frail-looking man
with ashy shoulder length hair a-scraggle,
sunken eyes, a hang-dog look —
but on stage, he transforms,
swells with power, inflated by the music
he pours himself into,
seated on rug'd floor, drawing up something
from beyond breath's bottom.

Gopalakrishnan: becoming
Krishna, Vishnu incarnate:
friend, lover,
goatherd, toddler,
never missing a beat
in the rhythms of time & condition,
the creative force,
maintainer, sustainer

Goplakrishnan:
attentive to the grinning mrdangumist
cradling his barrel drum, vibrationally
nurturing the blind violinist, giving them
all the play they need, pouring them tea
during blowing breaks,
touching them with eyes, hands, coaxing three plus
hours of ever expanding music,
lotus petals unfolding endlessly,
transforming each
before our own transforming
ii's.

"A musical architecture of precise forms"
classical ratios, golden means
to ends beyond
words & images —

       the blind man
led, feebly tottering, to his place,
aglow with vision,
the buck-toothed drummer with the not-quite-all-
there look:
on another plane

one rules the timeless heavens,
the other the ticking earth;

& Gopalakrishnan binds them in harmony,
breathes life
through his flute,
smiling at each, & us

something else at play as well

MA

When I came to you
I was but a seed
woven out of mystery
fashioned out of need
You fed me with your body
& you fed me with your mind
You were always there for me
You were always kind
   & no one
   but you
   would do
 & I knew

When I came to you
Everything was dark
You opened up my eyes
& you showed me how to walk
You showered me with kisses
& you bathed me with your tears
You ran your hands all over me
& washed away my fears
   & no one
   but you
   would do
 & I knew

When I came to you
I had never seen the light
I had only known the darkness
I had only known the night
You smiled the changing moon & stars
Then lifted up the sun
You showed me multiplicity
& then you showed me One
   & no one
   but you

would do
& I knew

When I came to you
You opened up your door
You gave me all your riches
& you offered me more
You gave me a map
& you gave me a key
You held me so close to you
& then you set me free

   & no one
   but you
   would do
& I knew

NURTURE / NATURE

offering
what is needed

a little water
a sunny smile
a touch
a caring word

nurturing

we are
most human
most humble
most god-like

HERACLITIS GOT IT RIGHT
    (notes on the flood of '93)

We were on dry land but
the river was in the air around us,
thick & humid. As dusk blended to night,
it dampened the seats of an open windowed car.
You couldn't see it, but the river was in the cracks
& grumblings of thunder, in the dark brows
& churning stomachs of clouds; invisible,
it was in the parks & woods &
marshes along the shore,
in the fields farmers plowed, in the green
life spinning out toward the sun, in the gray faces
of the boulders & the cliffs, & in the dark
caves burrowing inward.
Impalpable, the river was in the houses
that perched in its sight,
it washed imperceptibly over
the proud bridges & the confident roads.
For some time now the river had withdrawn
its attention, but it hadn't
             relinquished its claim.

        ◆

It was simply inhaling, taking stock
of itself, taking its
time.

You couldn't exactly define
the river, certainly not
as its usual channel. It was too alive
to be captured in such caricature,
too rich not to be more
complex.
      You couldn't control,
you couldn't contain, you couldn't take

89

for granted, no matter how hard you tried,
no matter how softly

you let the river lull you
over the years, no matter how you sang its praise,
no matter how you hyped its land, its views,
no matter how high, how hopefully, how hard
you dammed its persistence;
no matter how you tried to sandbag
its desires.

    The river was too alive to be
unchanging; Heraclitis got it right: *you couldn't
step into the same river twice;*

it was bound
to express
                its expansive nature
from time to time.

       ◆

    Never argue
with a river. Better poets than I have
compared it to an ancient god. Wherever
the gods are — brother, sister — respect them.
Spit at the heavens, the proverb says,
& you spit in your own face.
Reflect on this,
this poet says: the same thing
happens when you spit in the river.

      ◆

Let us then give praise to the river.

Let us make offerings, our animals, our cars,
our homes, our lives, our various
baseball card collections.
For the river came down to us
from the highest places, yea, the very heavens,
it rose up to swallow us whole.
This engulfing river tip-toeing up the steps
of the Gateway Arch to the West, this river
is all rivers. This disorderly flowing
oneness, this carrier of flotsam & waste,
this is the sacred Ganges, pouring down through
Shiva's dreaded hair, to devour,
to nourish, to shape, to revise this onflowing
poem, to curse, & to bless.

◆

Something imperturbable about the rise of a river.
A majestic calm to meditate upon,
(if it weren't so life threatening).

◆

Sometimes the river flashes fiercely
& springs like a cat.

But now the river offers time,
intense geological time,
to reflect,
to consider what to do,
where to go,
what to take with you,
& what
to leave behind.

◆

Measure
time in space

of inevitability
& inches.

The rise is slow.

Why are we here?

The river compels us to look
at the question rising
with the waters
now seeping through
our futile walls,
the boundaries between us.

What can we do?
The river compels us to look
to ourselves, to each other.

◆

Maybe we're all drowning
in slow motion
in the thick air.

ANOTHER SONG FOR ORPHEUS

Orpheus' song could charm the birds,
the beasts, the trees.
His verbal/vocal magic even charmed death itself
whose shadowy god permitted him
to descend to the Underworld
& bring back Eurydice, his love. Or so Orpheus
thought. We know
the story.
Orpheus the singer returned alone.

But the point is, he returned. Back from grave Hades.
Back from the dead.
Returned the same,
but different.

If only Orpheus hadn't looked back. Had kept his
living breath
on creation, on the next line
of the tale he was spinning,
on the outward unfolding
of the verse, on the burst
from the seed of unraveling stem

If only he'd ridden that green rhythm faithfully
toward the brimming light & succeeded
& brought back into the world, with him,
revived, renewed, Eurydice, his love.

But Orpheus the singer turned, & lost
the thread, found himself
in a dark sinkhole of desire
where memory was too strong. Too deeply rooted.
Love lived there.
Fear of loss.
Death.
Eurydice.

& Orpheus turned, turned
back, out of love,
dead in his tracks,
committed to memory,
marking time.

 In the stillness,
Orpheus the singer
couldn't grasp the ghost
couldn't hold love's memory, death, in that dark pit
of mind. His footing wasn't sure enough,
sure enough,
in those uncertain depths.

& so, in a sense
(innocence) he fell, fell in love, fell deeper
than the most probing rooted strand,
fell ephemeraly, eternally
with Eurydice
all tangled up
in the holy
grasp of death.

◆

But Orpheus returned, I said.
He returned with the spears of grass,
the bursts of weeds & flowers.
Returned alone,
the same, but different.

Orpheus returned,
returned to sing,
to be surrounded by love,
& torn apart by it.

And we return to him, turning back
to stories that describe us

what we reach for in darkness,
the bliss we can't hold on to,
the past that shapes us,
& leaves us
the same, but different.

CAN'T HOLD ON

All I've ever said
All I've ever done
All I've ever wanted

gone   gone

All I've ever had
All I've ever won
All I've ever needed

gone   gone

Gone like breath the changing wind
Bone to dust where once was skin
Won't ever be the same again

gone   gone
can't hold on

Gone are all the selves I've been
Gone are those who once were kin
Gone like breath the changing wind

gone   gone
can't hold on

(gate gate paragate
parasamgate bodhi svaha!)

gone   gone
can't hold on

If you're proud
Catch a cloud

gone   gone
can't hold on

    If you're a giver
    Bring me a river

gone   gone
can't hold on

    If you dare
    capture the air

gone   gone
can't hold on

    If you'd be higher
    Hold on to fire

gone   gone
can't hold on

    At your birth
    Root in the earth

gone   gone
can't hold on

(gate paragate
parasamgate bodhi svaha!)

All the dues I've ever paid
All the music that I've played
All the love I've ever made

gone   gone
can't hold on

Gone are all the selves I've been
Gone like breath the changing wind
Won't ever be the same again

gone gone
can't hold on

A POET WHO DIED YOUNG
for Arthur Brown (1947-1982)

he knew the song the goldfish sang
in his window world, the slow ripple
of a lover, the sad, triumphant music
of the caged bird

he knew & reached through
the window, the world, the cage
of the body, writing
a bop kaballah on the empty notebook pages

writing out of junebug flashings
noting the differences between cement & concrete,
growling out belly blown improvisations
terrablue afternoons,
blowing the logic of the gone
Buddy Bolden's trumpet, the preacher's
clean scat, Mr. Parker's precise needling

What could language do
    to cut through
itself
    ?

He knew his job was to poet:
the words spoke through him, from all over
through time too, when he was really there, ready,
in the flow, when the words were heady &
moist in the corners of his mouth

    then it was *nothing but love*
nothing but love —

& he knew then
he was immortal & that he was destined
to die
        with a lopsided smile like Michaelangelo

on his scaffold

& he thought
death might not be
      all that bad

except for the living

STRANGE DAYS

Strange days of March between Winter & Spring.
A death. A burial. White gloved black Masons
intone ancient ritual over black man in white coffin.
Unending prayer trails off as top-hatted leader still
talking & walking . . .
leads his troops away. Walking & talking.
Life trails away. . .
Prayers answer prayers like echoes
in the dim chapel light.
We're alone with our dying.

Worms &
grandchildren among the remains. Tiny crocus buds
signaling in the garden. Icy puddles
in the graveyard we're walking through.
Watch your step.
Bow your head before the etched name.
Place a stone.
I was here.

AT TAGORE'S DEATHBED

Navigating the rush-hour crowds of Calcutta,
the din of horns & hawkers, the excavated streets
thick with puddles of rubble,
cows & their droppings,
beggars hunched on sidewalk squares, & workers
wending home;
hopped a bus & stood in its stifling heat, hanging on
for dear life as it jerked & pulled & willed its way
along, through the resistant, impossible city
of your birth, Tagore; leaped off,
then walked some more.
Dr. Datta, thin Virgil, beside me, talking non-stop,
serenely, all the way, of you, beloved bard of Bengal,
whose *songs still sing*, & keep you alive in this state,
this infernal, vibrant metropolis, your city, your
world--Datta knew you
at *Shantihniketan*, Peace House,
your ashram school in the countryside,
whose only walls were sky, whose chalk was moon
& sun, & blackboard night &
monsoon clouds; & like a Bengali,
he loved you dearly.
We looked at the photos
in the gallery of your family home,
now a seedy arts college,
in the space where starry nights your
musical dance-dreams were first performed-
youthful you as Valmiki,
outlaw turned poet;
you with politicians, philosophers,
writers — in China, London, Iraq; you prematurely
patriarchal; you with your wife, who died
halfway through your years; you with Einstein,
you with the man-miracle you named
Mahatma — you with your white Whitmanic
beard flowing

over the planet, everywhere & nowhere,
formless & familiar
as your *Brahmo* god — Valmiki, you wrote,
was moved by the singing & suffering of the hunted,
haunted birds to abandon banditry & become a bard;
& Walt, your American uncle, & my you, too
became a poet
out of the cradle endlessly rocking, responding
to a solitary winged singer
trilling freely, feelingly
for his departed mate. Datta says
this tragic sense
is what makes the poet.
This, no doubt, & . . .
                              words.

We wound up at your deathbed, Tagore,
as the lights were being turned out
all around us; finally, in the dusk,
Datta & I shared a silent moment
meditatively with you —

                    then a flock of birds, black
kites, burst against the sky, with cries
raucous as downtown Calcutta, & one
settled on the sill, peered in curiously,
intelligently, I thought, & then
flew off, into the emptiness
                              to sing,
to sing, I imagined,
                         like you, Tagore,
as Datta smiled, & my solitary heart
fluttered

WORD SWORD

```
         w
         o
         r
         d
w o r d s w o r d s w o r d s w o r d s w o r d s w o r d s
         w
         o
         r
         d
```

FOOL POEM # 1
for poets

Here we go with another
session
   pounding keys as if
to re-shape them to fit
   supple locks, & open
stubborn doors.
   O god!
the futility & the vanity
   of such an effort at dis-
covery!
   Tripping
over one's own shadow
   trying to pound
 even from sound
the stone's blood.
   Always the image
 of the Fool dances by,
some cuddly hellhound yapping
   at his heels,
   the canyon

yawning

SO LONG

fool, fool,
bent like a gnome
fool, fool,
writing the poem
fool, fool,
wants to go home

i been a fool too long too long
i been a fool too long

fool, fool,
mirror mutters
fool, fool,
student stutters
fool, fool
lover sputters

i been a fool too long too long
i been a fool too long

fool, fool,
fool day & night
fool, fool's
gold shining bright
fool, fool,
an apple says 'Bite'

i been a fool too long too long
i been a fool too long

fool, fool,
cool & calm
fool, fool,
dreaming the bomb
fool, fool,
meaning no harm

i been a fool too long too long
i been a fool too long

fool, fool,
a look in the eye
fool, fool,
born to die
fool, fool,
wondering why

i been a fool too long too long
i been a fool too long

DAN DE LION

you used to stand so straight
so bright & light just like the sun

now so soon yr stooped & pooped
all frail & gray

& gone
to seed

CHILI-MAC
for Allen Ginsberg (1926-1997)

Poets want Irv's Good Food
not because of the sight rhyme
but because this is a real diner,
white tiled exterior
& spinning counter stools
the last of a dying breed
in South St. Louis.

Greasy menus,
Nehru capped cook,
lone gray waitress,
wino's & investment brokers
all bow & nod
to thy egalitarian fare.

A genuine place.
Bus stop pacers get invited in
out of the cold.
Everyone knows everyone — if you're new
you're soon known. No need
to introduce yourself.
Irv & his crew will name you.
          Ginsberg
came in & tried the Chili-Mac Special,
grilled the cook
about how to make it,
for who, & why.
Is it popular? The interrogation
went on & on. Social
research.
It all boiled down
to three words.

Cheap and Filling.

Allen looked at me.

More for less, I said.
Like good poetry, he smiled.

We ordered some & it filled the bill.
More American than apple pie.
Yankee Doodle's Italian pasta,
the feather in his cap,
tickling Native American beans & peppers.
Multi-cultural dialogue afloat
in the gastric juices.
Irv asked, *Is it good?*

It was a good year
before I needed to go back.
Allen long gone
from Burroughs' home town.

I walked in the door & was greeted like a regular.
"Howyadoin Bud?" said the chef.
"Well, well, well. Mr. Budget."
chimed in the waitress.
"Where's Mac?" the chef asked.
I looked at him weird.
"You know,
your friend with the beard," he said.
"Chili-Mac."

MANGIA ITALIANO WITH STEVE
for Steven Pitters

south side cheap pasta eats
at mangia italiano
waiting for the open mike performance bards
to begin their rites — home made noodles
& healthy sauces, salads, all you can eat, less than
five bucks, a good deal
meal; restless energy of high-schoolers on up
rollicking in the narrow aisles.
From my table through the front glass window I see
two teens lighting a joint; nerdy kids
burst through the aisles
to hug & shriek at one another,
restless, sexual, a simulated high
to be *not* alone,
in not out — the first
poem's about a cop killer —
"he did it, didn't give a shit"
the twenty something poet is pushing it,
screaming over the mike,
but no one's listening
too hard, some
not at all
that poetry might be
the shove of personality; a slightly ill
control of the technological, not technical control
of the illogical; amplification not implication;
instead of
an imposing electric voice
a voice imposing itself by electrically enhanced
volume, i.e., in my face — hadn't counted on
that direction
the poet booms on, a poem
for "the homeless", for "love", for or against
the "suits" & "robots" swivelling in big chairs
in antiseptic offices; the particular

however, unseen — the reality cops
        walk in, anonymously alerted, two,
a man & woman, crisply uniformed, each
only a few years older than the high-schooler heads
they recoil, walkie-talkies blaring
not unlike the unheard poetry, but the cop
poem's over, the dope's already copped, the back
room's empty
& in the sudden hush
                        no one knows nothing & I say
X generation misfits, yuppie dropouts, big booming
babies, afficionados
of some mediated get-a-life nostalgic sixties never-
lived, some cool
jeans commercial, turn off
the tv in your brains — put out your own antennae —

        write about clinking coffee cups
& cops silencing poets

the best line of the night's
from a musician playing saying
"free music, the only music
that's worth it"

FAME

The Qutab tower, 'the symbol of Delhi,"
Mr. Joshi says,
stands brazenly, 70 meters high, marking
Islam's conquest, & immortalizing
the ruler who built it
whose name I forget.
Built it on the site, literally on top of Hindu temples:
smashed the trunks off the faces of the elephant god,
Ganesha; smashed the smiles & breasts of the *yakshi*
women clinging to its base;
no idols for this prudent dude, just a stony erection.
& across the way, his successor tried to outdo him,
build a higher tower, get remembered longer.
But "man proposes, God disposes," Mr Joshi says.
What you see is a squat, stubby mockery of the first.

Story is, this moghulish *macher* went out one day
to admire the progress of his tower tomb.
A workman high above, perhaps made jittery
by the static of vibrations
beaming from below, dropped a brick
momentum-usly down
upon his august presence,
nailed the *wazir*
upside the head,
& crushed him in his tracks.

They buried the deceased modestly.

No one bothered to finish the tower.

POEM FOR A PALM LEAF PAINTER

We met on the steps
of Konarak's Temple of the Sun
in the jungly lushness of Orissa.

After I followed you with my mind
you followed me with your feet.
                    Got around

to showing me your wares.
            We bargained hard,
struck a deal for your palm leaf painting of Ganesha,

Shiva's son, elephant-headed boy-god,
            overcomer of obstacles,
surrounded by ten circles
bearing Vishnu's incarnations:

a fish, a turtle, a wild boar, a dwarf,
Rama with an axe, the other Rama
with a bow, flute-tooting Krishna, Buddha

beneath umbrella, jug-eyed Jugger Naut, Jag Nath —
you named them all — including Kalki, a riderless
horse with flaming candle
burning on its back, transformer of energies,

the avatar to come.

We talked beneath the elevated statue of
the evening sun
hundreds of feet above us
on the pyramidic steps

serene & bronzed, dusky Surya looked
perhaps a little weary; below the sun god,
& above us, gigantic erotic sculptures:

couples coupling,
cunnilingaling — athletic, acrobatic,
creative, voluptuous, sublime.

Your flowing black hair, painted forehead, dark eyes,
wild smile, reminded me of jazz musicians I've
known & blown with, dear friends on the other side

of the planet, home.
It was important to you that I understood
you weren't just some hustling hack, that you read

the *Gita* every day, learned the stories
behind the images, chanted the mantras,
tapped the *shakti* force to feed your art & soul.

Not the greatest artist, you admitted, but sincere.
You told me with hands & words you played flute
like Lord Krishna, knew time

on tabla & mrindangum like the *Nataraj*
god dancing life, even blew an unimaginable sax
(I could hear it as some otherworldly Bird).

Underneath your painting's incarnations
on their worlds of palm-leaf flaps
line drawings, humans, underlying

their deific covers
men & women making love, like
the stony figures lording over us,

kama sutra poses,
beneath the images of gods.
        Beneath the ledges, art,

                you shrug,
& smile, hands up, to signify . . .

nothing. . . a trifle . . . a gesture

tripping

    "something
out of nothing: an exchange
    of energy," me thinking, "mind

& matter, spirit & body,
   will & act,
     inspiration & realization"

really wailing now, your hands
    & halting words provoking
    this racing mental babble.

   "Exuberance is Beauty," I exclaim,
quoting Blake, this poet's guru,
   out of Western left field.

"Play of God," you reply,
   not missing a beat, *"Shiva-shakti,"*
"om mani padme hum" (the jewel is in the lotus)

these wild rhapsodic outbursts
dissolve
into silent waves

of sound
  & heat
    & light

radiant, pregnant, words
floating in the air

over the language barrier,
crossing culture's gap —

   playful

attraction

fills the mysterious
emptiness

sculpts the space
      about us

shapes the paint on palm leaf
      held in the palm of my hand —

      our eyes dance

& suddenly, in the wide
      silence, connecting

inside & out
above & below

we meet,

a single mind,
on stony ancient steps,
before we part

FIGURES

1 + 1
is sum
  X
  1

1 + 1
  is
even
  2

it's odd
  that
  3

can be

  1
  2

THE SAINT & THE MISSION

In the great courtyard
of the San Juan Bautista Mission
flowers still grow, along with scented herbs;
bees still buzz their flight patterned language,
dipping into flowers' bright petal cushions
to sit in meditative silence, sipping honeyed bliss;
the birds still soar & flap, singing songs of longing
beneath the vast & soothing sky still a gleaming
blue; the hills still spread & ripple in all directions
shaping this verdant valley,
cupping this serene & holy spot
like prayerful hands, inverted,
as if gathering clear water
for unseen lips.
In this valley, on these pathways,
through this courtyard
Fray Junipero Serra walked 200 years ago, walked
from the chapel
to the music room & stopped, to listen to the sounds
as he sat on these stone garden benches drinking in
the ubiquitous beauty with all his open senses.

The kiss of the Sun for Pardon
The Song of the Birds for Mirth
One is nearer God's heart in a Garden
Than anywhere else on Earth

reads a sign for the tourists who walk these paths
in increasing numbers now
that Fray Serra has been nominated for sainthood.

I wander these intoxicating garden grounds
in the warm sun, hearing no birds,
lost in my head & time,
wondering what Fray Serra prayed for.
Did he pray for the success of this

& the other outposts
he established up & down California's rugged coast?
for the monks & the drunks that they sheltered?
Did he
pray for the souls of "my"
mission Indians
who worked the surrounding fields
& fed this holy flock?
Did he show his "red heathens" open Christian love?
or Inquisitive close-minded severity?
Or a measure of each?

Did Fray Serra pray for forgiveness
in front of these bright multi-colored flowers?
Or later, alone, in front of a statue,
in his dark chapel?
Did he pray for each of the four
thousand three hundred red souls
who resisted slavery & salvation?

Four thousand three hundred
red souls battered & murdered on these grounds,
broken bodies buried in a mass grave
beneath the serene surface,
under the dirt floor
of a barren corner room
where no plaques offer poems,
no windows let in light.

Did the saint turn the other cheek
to the sight of their suffering
or, drawing the bow across his cello, nod,
& consign them to the pit?
What voice spoke to him, spoke through him
in this garden?

A Vatican spokesman
denied the floggings, the forced labor,
the massacre: "No one

is beatified if there is a shadow
of a doubt about his virtue."
But there are only shadows
in the empty corner room, swirling
shadows where boarded windows allow little light,
shadows blanketing the bare dirt floor, over the mass
grave at the San Juan Bautista Mission.

LOGGING COUNTRY

At the Bluebird Cafe
  the coffee cups are clacking &
everybody's talking bout the accident
yesterday on 101, one of
those big tractor-trailers
overturned,

"held up Ed for an hour."

"That's the best-behaved group of rubbernecks
I ever worked with."

The battered baseball cap
  bobbing up & down
  the gray trucker's
          beating gums weighing
                  relative
          highway bloodstains

on the next stool,
                young Tom, jobless at 9:40, looks
disheveled & beat — muddled
as Edna the cook
                leans through her window
from the kitchen, & hisses
          a stage whispery steam
                    towards his ear

i.e. from the grill
          to the grilling — Tom
      shakes
  his sorry head,
              his cigarette ash,
      the jar of sugar

      we order eggs "over-easy"

from name-pinned Claudette, wise-apple
waitress, shot through
     the empty picture frame
   to the receded Edna, Claudette commanding—
     "over easy Bluebird style,
with a run in it—"

 "yeah," Edna crackles back
over frying bacon,
                         to no one in particular,
"we give it to you fast—
     the way it is."

                         "Management Policy"
streaked with grease, hung over
Tom's counter-cradled head:

                         "This is *not* Burger King.
                         We don't do it your way.
We do it *our* way."

Strangely,
               before coffee is even served,
                    the morning clarifies

AFTER VALLEJO

Idle on a stone, unemployed,
He looks into the river . . . Narcissus
Of scrounge, fop of scruff, suit shiny
at elbow & butt, what creature stares up,
wizened & tight-lipped, out of the deep?
Having devoured the short ends of cigarettes
& the smoke of the soul, having walked through
the classifieds, "Full of jobs,"
says the President, "full of . . ."
having stood in the lines of the jobless multitudes,
having filled out the forms full of the routine questions
requiring routines for answers—Who *are* you? Who are *you*?
A man whose newspaper covers his head in the rain,
who traces the lines of his face in the mirror,
lines written by this tragic poetry;
a man who stoops over in a phone booth's privacy
to count his change & cough,
who haunts the harsh streets, the hiring hall warehouses,
the coffee shops of oblivion.
Idle on a stone, unemployed.
Home is no longer home, as I am no longer I.
Who will offer the rag he needs to mop his brow?
Who will fill the cavity that aches his spirit?

What will the river say?

And what are
his qualifications?
Three million years spent
developing an opposable thumb, an upright posture.
A couple of million thinking, abstracting,
Hundreds of thousands traveling, learning, adapting
to arrive precisely here.
(Only a few thousand learning to write—
Don't hold it against him.
He can dig ditches, push paper, build pyramids.

He has invented sources of light, a certain smile,
a simple mirror.

Where will he go?
What will he do?
How will he fill out
his application? Can he
sign in under 'Last Job,'
"helped a guy?"

Will he beg? Will he steal?
Or will he stay still, by the flowing river,
idle on a stone, unemployed?

PISSING IN THE GUTTER
(a poem full of ugly words in praise of Beauty)

We would interrupt the game of "Johnny Fuck!"
to piss in the gutter. Watching the streams of urine
fountaining in beautiful arcs and washing the filth
gathered along the curb downhill toward the sewer.
Johnny Fuck was a simple game, a variation on tag
adapted to the four box wide sidewalk —
the two outer regions represented "shore,"
the two inner ones the "river"
territory of Johnny Fuck — players would chant
"Johnny Fuck! Johnny Fuck! may I cross your river?"
& "Fuck" would reply, *"not unless you wear the color
       !"*
(& he'd name his pleasure, the price of permission).
Those who could show the designated hue on their
public outer
or private innerwear, could float across free,
those who didn't had to negotiate his patrol,
trying to elude JF's Loch Ness Monster tag. If
touched, you became "It."
The best part of the game was the profane chant, the
thrill of ritually uttering the forbidden, power-
charged language.
"Johnny Fuck! Johnny Fuck!" Sounding it still
gives me perverse pleasure:
Beseeching chant, ugly as sin, I, too,
proudly projected
to appease the Lord of the River.

And the forbidden act of pissing in the gutter
naturally accompanied this artless pastime, relieving
its boring repetition, its unique tension,
with release. Toeing our concrete shoreline,
River of Fuck to our rear,
ocean of gutter before us, our penises
bared to the summer

air, the exhaust of blind sloopy traffic on Seaman
Avenue, touching ourselves
with the vision of a self-generated
beauty! — from all that
was designated dirty & ugly.

Bubbles bursting in the curbside stream.
Flowing downhill.

A yellow river for Johnny Fuck.

BAMBOO
for Jomo

We sit on the curb under the highway overpass
like three old winos, watching the rain pour down,
drinking beer, enjoying
the cool breeze — Uncle Dan advising young Jomo
on the craziness of the world, corrupt city politics,
smoking & drinking ("don't wind up like me")
the rain pounds down, floods & rushes
through the gutters.
Dan invites Jomo to go to the track with him
the next day,
describes the people there with their
prodding probing fingers
demanding cigarettes, money, contact:
"You should go once & you should go with me. . ."
He tells Jomo about the value of friends,
about the times he had no place, but always had
a friend's home to crash:
how "the only thing your dad has
that I don't is you. . . & that's a lot. . ."
The words come out in a torrent
tells him how much he loves him, how
if anything happened to him,
how much it would hurt

Jomo listens, drinks it all in:
the evening suddenly cooled
the ozonish blanket of thick heat finally blown away
the baseball game long over, the bars, blues,
2 am gutter reveries
in the wind
renewing, cleansing,
driving rain
memory seeds already stirring. . .
the movement from childhood to adulthood
before us

in these moments, under the overpass,
avuncular, toothless Danny,
me as square pops,
Jomo . . .

I watch my son,
I am without words; they are unnecessary.
He is like a shoot of bamboo creaking in the forest

GRANDFATHERS

One chain-smoked cigarettes,
rolled his own
with slow deliberate movements,
never wanted matches,
lit each new smoke
with the butt of the last.

Worked as caretaker
for a club of rich French
& German businessmen
in Salonika,
by the Aegean Sea,
where he watched
the Greeks & Turks unite
to drive out the Bulgarians.
They'd shoot at
the Bulgarians,
driving them back,
street by street.
Then they'd shoot at
each other.

Like most who lived there,
this grandfather
didn't give a damn
who won, when the smoke
cleared.
But the Germans,
the Germans cared,
& so they tried out their bombers
over the city, warming up
for 'The Great War.'

The city smoked
with this grandfather.
But each work day

ended the same way for him.
He'd sweep up his own butts,
throw them away in the trash
& consign the pile to flames.

He was a disgrace
to the family,
for he worked on the Sabbath.

His grandfather
had been head rabbi
in Palestine,
& his brother
was a rabbi in Salonika,
& a money-changer
on the side —
working out of a little booth
on a busy corner.
My father,
who became a grandfather,
remembered it well.

This changeling brother
was thought highly of
by the family.
But my grandfather,
the black sheep, swept
& saved his money.
He left for America by steamship
with his wife & oldest sons, Alberto & Arturo,
to keep the boys from being drafted.

My father, the grandfather,
the orphaned twelve year old son,
stayed behind with his sisters,
slept five in a bed
with uncles & cousins & aunts,
& sold needles & postcards & thread
to soldiers' outstretched hands

through barbed wire fences.

He was in Salonika
during the Great Fire of 1917.
He saw British troops,
a few blocks ahead of the blaze,
spraying buildings in the Jewish quarter
with gasoline.
They preferred to destroy the city
than to let the Germans have it.
Jews jumped into the harbor
to escape the conflagration.

All that smoke.

When my father came to America
he took up cigars,
& eventually opened a cigar store
on Chambers Street,
near the Immigration Bureau.
His grandfather, the chain-smoker,
died of Nazi gas,
age 101.

Smoke was everywhere.

On the other side,

my mother's father
was from Jannina,
from an ancient line of Greek Jews.
In America, this grandfather
worked in a cigarette factory
& lived in Harlem.
He is best remembered
for his big, beautiful brown eyes
& for the love he showered on his wife,
his three children,
& even on distant relatives

emerging from steerage
on fogbound Ellis Island.
He died young, coughing,
in the influenza epidemic of 1919,
two years after Salonika went up in smoke.

Heartsick, my grandmother followed
six months later, dying
before her children's eyes
on a borrowed cot

For years
my mother thought the "deathbed"
was a special bed
people brought in for the dying.

All those babushka'd aunts
& kimona-peddling uncles
wept at the funerals,
but none took in the children.

Somehow my mother, the grandmother,
survived, taking care
from age ten
of her two younger brothers,
not letting anyone break up the family,
shifting from foster home
to foster home
& back again
to the Hebrew Orphan Asylum.

She met my cigar-smoking father,
married, &
just after his father (my grandfather) &
about the time his chain-
smoking grandfather died,
made him a son.
The son worked in the smoke shop,
handed over Turkish

blend Camels
to hacking chain-smokers
(old proverb of Salonika Jews,
"The camel doesn't see his own hump")
swept up their butts
as they disappeared down Broadway
in their own smoke,
didn't smoke cigarettes, cigars,
didn't think he knew
his own grandfathers;
but carried on,
imagined them
as incense smoke curled
in the lamplight, wondered;
eventually
married, became a father
of a son; a grandfather
of grandsons in the hazy future;

> lit a candle, a joint,
> watched the smoke rise,
> linger around the ceiling;
> it vanished into thin air,
> except for what remained
> inside him

POEM FOR GRANDMA

The room was dark & full of musty furniture,
plush, velvety, worn armchairs,
a velour couch
draped with the lacy yellowing
doilies she embroidered,
bowls filled with sucking candies
on every surface,
a sense of the grave closing in,
the sun banished
for some unseen offense.
Somewhere in the Bronx, circa 1950.
The radio abuzz with guys, like my father, named Joe
DiMaggio, McCarthy, G.I. (& only last week,
I met a Cheyenne Indian who said,
"My name's Joe,
but call me Angel. Too many 'Joes' in this world, not
enough 'Angels'").
She came from Ios, the island
where Homer was born, or so the story goes, as
Rebecca tells it.
              She was a Romaniot,
who Grandpa had to teach Ladino.
Got out of Salonika
before the Great Fire set by the British
destroyed the Jewish quarter, before the Turkish
bombings, before World War I, before
the Holocaust, before
all her children.

From that clear Greek birthlight
to smoky steerage, Harlem, another
language (she'd teach him), another walkup
cave on another island, another
beginning to manage: brisses & weddings,
the complexities of lives
              never fully here;

       & the burial arrangements, remembering . . .
       the passage . . .
of time, each moment a gravestone
knocked over, a piece of candy offered
to sweeten the conversation,
       the accented word
exhaled into the traffic's exhaust,
a stitch in the tapestry, steady
gnarling hands
barely moving in the dimness,
slipping the needle in
& out, & later, lighting
yartzite candles, dark-eyed wrinkles
turning back, & squinting, to see
the pattern.

   Dusk
in the worn plush Bronx, alone,
toothless, still squinting

(outliving the others),
in this oppressive shade. Lucky
to be an immigrant smile slowly woven
through New York's patchwork bustle.
       A fixed jaw. A crack
       in the drawn curtains of
the twentieth century.
A patch of light on the drab dusty rug.
An imperious, stubborn strength
beaming down
on her little grandchild.

Michael

VIGIL

When I was six I bet my cousins which elevator
would go higher, faster. We stood together
before hermetically sealed doors, & rooted

for arrows gauging an ascent,
swinging horizon to horizon,
cheered gazing upward
watching numbers ticked off

as on a sped up semi-circular clock, arrows whizzing
like real time as you get older,
past the floor where our grandmother lay dying;

& on, upwards
toward the hospital's heavenly penthouse,
which neither
pneumatic chariot of our racetrack imaginations

ever quite reached
before plunging precipitously
toward the grandstand lobby where we stood,
& lower

to subterranean floors, mysteries, depths.
Grandma lay dying.
We didn't know what to think, or feel,
or cheer about that.

Better not even to watch, mesmerized,
on the ground floor, by a sense of the eternal
up & down motion of life

SONNET 4-D FOR BLACK HOLE LOVE

Black Hole Sunshine, lighting dark life, kindle
These embers tickling my soul like bitter ash.
Your event horizon's too hot to handle,
Yet, drawn to your singularity, I'm cold as cash.

Black Hole Sunshine, you compress energies
Like proverbial camels
passing through needles' eyes.
These together vibrations suggest synergies
Beyond anything I've up to now realized.

Black Hole Sunshine, your beams
leave my vessels shattered,
Your divine sparks spill all over, yes,
I've fallen for you.
& so, from on my knees,
here's what light I've re-gathered,
Poured into your *ginnunga gap*
to shade your black blue.

(Mocking matches lit to mystery,
worthless words of spaced out rhyme;
Mad meters measuring endlessness, as we ache &
break thru time)

138

THE CREED OF THE SEED

How something so BIG
comes from something so little
A seed is the material form of need
Each of us was once a seed

A seed with a plan
to become a human
that grows & needs
& breeds its own seeds

with plans of their own
to become fully grown

need, urge
constriction, surge
inhale, ex,
attraction, sex

seeds alight
feeling all right
taking hold
as they unfold

& so it goes, on & on
life just flows, eon to eon

all those seeds, with all their needs
all of life just breeds & feeds

creating motley earth's
unrelenting birth

& so something so BIG
comes from something so little
& the need in the seed's
at the heart of the riddle

MOON IN PISCES

Moon in the water.
A thousand ripples.

Constantly changing faces
mirror the same face.

JIM AIGOE'S SATORI

cottonwood trees
   wind —
      Shhhhh

WARRIOR POET

I am Poet-General of the Army of Love.
My uniform is my human skin.
My shining medals are my eyes.
With concentrated effort
I deploy my forces:
Breath, Words, Poems.
We are prepared for Struggle.
We sail the Cosmic Sea.
We fly the sky of Vision.
We ride the curvy currents of Time & Space.
Alighting, we advance toward you:
Dancing to the beat of the Heart;
Shocking & awing with explosions of Spirit;
Breath propelling at lightning speed
Words precise & deadly,
Poems fueled by the Soul's nuclear power
Invasive weapons of Mass Conjunction.

The super weapon: a still, small voice
Penetrating your defenses.

Surrender your self!
Victory!
Ah!

VOICES IN MY HEAD
for Ira Cohen (1935-2011)

It's hard job being a poet,
I hear Ira saying, in my head,
some say you're a medium,
for God, for the collective consciousness,
or unconscious, it's hard
bearing that weight, facing those things,
frankly, no one else wants to
give a shit about,
            Ira Cohen is rasping
in my head,
what's in his head, the head
of a poet, the aching head singing & shrieking
praises & alarms
for life under fire,
as it dances,
like Shiva in his flaming ring,
I'm feverish, my head is ringing,
this poet's head
silent too long, bereft of song
till now when the cacophony
of voices is too much, the phony *caca*
of life on the planet under fire
cannot defy description any longer
or we'll all be consumed
as the bullshit ignites
engulfing the supermarkets
the dwarf of ignorance
is dancing on our temples
making them throb, a poet's voice
is in my head, Ira Cohen,
a tongue in my ear, wondering
what Laura Bush is dreaming, before
turning channels; Max Schwartz on the line
from Sacramento, improvising in my ear
because Attila Jozsef from Hungary

is in both our heads, & he too knows
"It isn't me that shouts, it's the world that rumbles,"
the world that drives you mad,
("drive," Creeley sd, my teacher
who's also in my head, *"for Christ's sake,*
look out where you're going,"
& he responding to Dr. Williams, his teacher,
in his head, *"no one to witness & adjust,*
no one to drive the car – "), if you don't
hold on to the wheel,
the dharma, ill
fortuna can drive you,
like Attila, under the onrushing train,
call it the train of terror, call it greed, call it environmental
devastation, call it hatred, call it a bummer
relationship—I'm here to tell you
what the voices in my head are saying,
what they are praying as another spring
drifts toward summer, & George Bush sits
uncomfortably beside the bent Pope, like a schoolboy
called into the Principal's office, & the price of gasoline
is higher than ever, & we stay the course
denying what we know, the world is growing hotter
not warmer, the poet on the margins
of consciousness must shout to be heard, *it isn't me*
that shouts, it's the world that rumbles,
it's these voices in my head,
opening my heart to you, giving it words,
singing to its insistent beat

when the towers crumbled all that was left
was an empty space
ground zero
a dangerous place
a place of death
a hot place, full of embers & fire & ash,
a place of terror,
a place of love,
ground zero
an empty space on the horizon
as when God contracted,
zim-zum, sounds
a little like the sound of a plane honing in,
zim-zum, kaballah sez,
there was an emptiness too
an emptiness when God contracted
an emptiness
at the heart of things
an empty space at the center
of creation
once
there was unity
as in the garden
a sense of wholeness
the skyline was intact
zim zum changed things
the men used box cutters to take control
god contracted
disappeared from the center
hovered somewhere on the outside
while back amidst the rubble
they shouted his name in vain
saying
we'll never be the same again
the towers crumbled
flames flashed from windows on the other side

a light beamed out into
the newly created space
the vessels shattered
the terrible twos of the world
clashed like cymbals
thunder & lightning
the man & the woman
ran from the garden
covering themselves
amidst the shards, the shells
of what had been, amidst the sparks,
the embers,
a creation of sorts,
amidst the rubble
they set out,
& found out
where they were
ground zero

◆

i sit in my basement a week after the terror
a week after the declaration
we are at war
a week after & the rubble still smoldering
where the twin towers fell
a week later & i am back in my life
back writing on the blank screen
diving into my own empty center
trying to find
the word
diving inside to ground zero
a week later
trying to find god
in this dangerous smoldering place

NUCLEAR MADNESS

I
live under
the shadow of the bomb
I
live under
ground
Radio & television
buzzed
stay calm
& then
all hell
rained down

I
live under
the mushroom's head
Underneath
the twisted
roots
of trees
that withered
& shriveled up
dead
with forever
forbidden fruits

No one around me
knows
who to blame
Nobody
answers
why?

No one
can tell me
the score

or the game
Nobody sees
the sky

I
am a lucky one
buried alive
in this realm
of worms
& bones
One of the few
who
are lucky to survive
We make war now
with sticks
& stones

I
live under
the shadow of the bomb
in a shroudy
world
of night
I
live under
the mushroom's head
Nobody
sees
the light

Nobody
sees
the light

BLUE CURTAINS

First they covered up
the statue of Justice,
her naked truth
offensive,
her substantive body draped,
a tortured prisoner
struggling under wraps
behind the talking head
of dour Ashcroft's
pursed puritanical lips
announcing
his offensive
against our rights,
our Constitution; his U.S.
Patriot Act,
a refuge for scoundrels,
shielded from
Justice's body's critical gaze
by a blank blue curtain,
purchased at
a pretty price—

Then they covered up
Picasso's *Guernica*
behind the U.N. podium,
so Powell could bang the drum
for war without its
visual
commentary:
the rearing horse's ass
beside his head,
the writhing, agonized human
underfoot, the dumb,
brutal, blatant bull
lording over body parts,
the truth

of aerial bombardment & war
harshly lit
by bare
electric bulb
peering out over his shoulder
wouldn't do,
might temper
oily arguments —

blue curtain cover up
blue curtain universe
blue curtain reality

Bully Bush,
petulant & beady-eyed;
Bullet Headed Chaney,
gravely scowling,
radiating meanness;
reckless Rumsfield,
bellicosely blabbermouthing;
Dracula Wolfowitz
slavering on his pocket comb;
profiteering Perle;
wrongheaded Rice —

Wizards of Oz
behind blue curtains

chart the nation's course
through Hell —
                War,
deficits, empty language,
legalized torture, crucified truth, environ-
mental degradation,
crumbling schools, foreclosed homes,
metroplexes of the abandoned,
jobless teenagers
crowding bleak & broken streets
where recruiters prowl like roaches,

in search of fodder for more wars

so that millionaires
can become billionaires,
& prematurely old,
preternaturally cold
men can get their rocks off
in their all wet dreams
of world domination —

Bloodsuckers of the Economic Nightmare!
Torturers of the American Dream!

Victims left dangling on meat hooks on the wall.

First they covered up
Justice
& her naked truth,
then *Guernica*
& its horrors
& its light

behind blank blue
curtains

They drew the curtains,
blue curtains —
their curtains
curtains
for Justice, Truth
& Peace

COLLATERAL DAMAGE

Bomb a city to get one man.
Blow up a mountain to destroy a cave.
Use a howitzer to splatter a mosquito.
Burn down a haystack to find a needle.
Napalm a forest to turn over a new leaf.
Install Astroturf to get rid of the weeds.
Pollute the ocean to catch a fish.
Make enemies of your friends to get your enemy.
Poison the air to extract the oil.
Cancel the Constitution to defend the Constitution.
Tear open the ozone to fart out all your gasses.
Destroy the company to make sure you're paid millions.
Mangle the body to destroy a cell.
Kill all the dreams to snuff out a nightmare.
Fire the comedian to keep his jokes from getting serious.
Marginalize the poet & all the truth tellers.
Mangle the meanings to babel the language.
Dull all the senses so that nothing outrages.
Vaporize the checks! Stack the balances!
Destroy the village in order to save it.

Smash all the mirrors.

CRAZY WHITE MEN

who've never been to war
beat its drums
flapping their gums
a constant barrage of noise
all lips & teeth & bulging eyes
all foam & spittle
on every station
bloviating
to the nation

Crazy white men

who've never been to war
think they know the score
like how they must avert their eyes
when dropping terror from the skies
like how to muffle victims' cries
when posturing as if they're wise

Crazy white men

who've never been to war
love it from afar
like shrill drunks in a bar
picking fights with tired arguments
making little sense
lacking any evidence
denying any consequence

Crazy white men

who've never been to war
scream Saddam! Saddam!
scream Bomb! Bomb! Bomb!
scream Osama! Osama!
scream Bomba! Bomba! Bomba!

The monsters they themselves created
now they want incinerated

Crazy white men

who've never been to war
prey upon the poor
get off on giving orders
to others' sons & daughters
Who cares how many will come back
We need that oil from Iraq
& a pipe across Afghanistan
will make our President a man

a Crazy white man

who's never been to war
a total boor, a total bore
You come home from work
& listen to this jerk
Turn on your tv, get a beer,
sit in your chair
be numb, be dumb,
absorb the crazy white man rant
That's what the crazy white men want

Back to Manifest Destiny
It's everywhere on your tv

Don't ask for sense, don't ask for logic
You'll be called unpatriotic

SONG OF THE GOLDEN HARP

Nobody guarded the family jewels
the history of mankind,
the treasures of early civilization,
carted off the shelves, out of the cases.
Traffic jams of looters crept past smiling soldiers
in otherwise empty streets.
The lonely liberators stood within shouting distance
but ignored the cries for help
reverberating
from around the corner,
around the world.
The troops stayed put.
They ringed the oil ministry in bombed out Baghdad
& let the thieves have at the loot.

The golden harp will no longer play in public.
The song we hear over & over,
"Operation Iraqi Freedom,"
will lack accompaniment.

The lyrics empty as the museums.

TORTURER'S DEFENSE

We weren't the Libyan Secret Service.
We didn't break bones, burn flesh, yank out teeth.
We had well thought out methods.
Tried & true ones that never left a mark —
like waterboarding, popular during the Inquisition.
And we always kept a doctor nearby,
ready to perform an emergency tracheotomy
if the victim stopped breathing.
They call this torture?

Well thought out interrogation techniques
like sleep deprivation.
We never went longer than eleven days of this.

Hanging from the wall for a few days, freezing rooms,
incessant light, incessant loud music, locked in a box
with a bug we only said was poisonous & attacked the genitals.
We're not crazy.
We didn't think outside the box.

We stayed within carefully prescribed boundaries.
Maybe not those of that quaint document, the Geneva Convention,
but —
We had laws. We had rules. We had orders.
We had it from the very top.
We had God & freedom & right.
We had it all.

FLYING SHOES

The reporter threw his shoes at the President,
shouting: "This is your farewell kiss, you dog!
This is from the widows, the orphans,
& those killed in Iraq!"
The reporter was pummeled into submission,
jailed & tortured — & viewed around the world,
& especially in Iraq,
as a hero.

It was shoes' greatest moment
since Imelda Marcos's closet opened,
or since Khruschev pounded the podium
at the United Nations with his loafer
before retiring to write surrealist poetry

REFLECTIONS

Iraq
takes us back
to 'Nam.
Damn.

Strangers
in a strange land
make a stand
for what they claim
is grand.

Proved wrong
before long.
Yet deny
what's in front of every eye.
And the lessons of history
remain a mystery.

With each transparent lie
Thousands suffer, thousands die.

WAR NOTES

    1967:

steps of the Pentagon daylight vs. night
flowers down
the throats of rifles — weeping black marine — federal
marshals smashing
all the bottles off the ledge. Night — thinned crowd —
changing of the guard, weighted batons beating time
into white gloved palms, unsheathing of bayonets,
red eye of the tripoded camera, machine gunners on
the buildings' roofs, bleary morning eyes

    1989:

Tianammen Square — standing in front of the tanks
   flesh & bone, beating heart
 versus the inexorable advance
   of the Iron Age

        ◆

& Bush said:
   "Bring it on."

        ◆

   O War, what to say to your brute stare?
   Picasso snapped your picture, caught you
   as the bull raping Europa
      under naked electric light bulb,
      you looked up
   dumbly over the trampled bodies, over the
outstretched
    hand clutching a flower,
      alert & emotionless
      your bull's eye

scanned, as the bombers scan
         siting their targets
in the Arabian desert as I write; Goya
         traced your silent lines, War,
from the gently
sloping hillside, down the sword in its scabbard
& back
up & across the flashing rifle barrels
of the faceless firing squad
aiming at
         the outstretched victim, white-shirted,
bathed in light, splayed, face-twisted
with terror, not even a cross to prop him
against the fatal light
         that 3rd of May; *Newsweek* published
the suspected Vietcong's
         impromptu execution
by the pistol pointing chief of police
on Saigon's street,
         & "Apocalypse Now" staged the famous newsreel
footage
of your captain lighting the thatched roof
with his BIC,
         "destroying the village in order to save it."
O Poetry of War: Homer, Shakespeare,
Whitman, Crane, Remarque,
         Owen, Mailer, Blake's Gray
         Monk
all found words for you, deflated you
to your sad, complex
humanity" — the hermit's cry & the widow's
tear" — Heller saw your cruel absurdist Catch 22
Even I stood on your stony Pentagon steps
         & exorcised your demons,
stood staring into the eyes of your troops
in the bleak cold hours before dawn
         as if into a mirror: brother, enemy, self —
         War — Fear
         glistened back as we exchanged breaths,

& spent the chilly night together
futilely; a strange, strained intercourse: some stuck
daisies in your erect rifes, some tried to talk sense;
    sweet reason;
I found no words; you inspire, War, like love,
dumb awe. Perverse
    obsession.
But unlike love, War,
    you deny life

NEW ORLEANS BLUES
for Paul Thiel & Hari Sky Campbell

Crab legs, crawdads, gumbo & jambalaya
finger licking began here at the edge
of the swamp where alligators patrol
with periscope eyes, a city arose
like Jesus walking on water, performed
a balancing act, first line, a bobbing umbrella dance of life

The edge, the gulf, living below sea level,
the swamp, the winds, the rains, the driving
rain, the back & forth of the futile windshield wiper
in the stalled traffic, the crack of branches, electric wires —
where are we going? away, away, away, away,
I hear the windshield wiper say, but only it moves

I fell in love with you walking the streets of the French Quarter,
holding hands beneath the balustrades,
eating breakfast at our special place
on a side street never to be named, I fell in love with you sitting in
Louis Armstrong Park,
at the edge of the French Quarter, and then again nearby
in St. Louis #1 Cemetery
kissing among the mildewy crypts, I kept falling in love with you
in New Orleans, a kind of music filled me, I smelled mimosa

Everett Maddox, the sloshed poet in residence
at the Maple Leaf Bar,
raises his ghostly glass, hovering over the rising waters —
spirits wail in the wind, play tricks with peoples' minds,
clinging to a roof or to each other, all we have right here & now,
was that a gunshot? how will I get water? where's my little brother?
I hope & pray that they will never forget about me.

Do that step Mama Bailey
bring that blues boy down off that bandstand
he wants to join your circle — do that first lining,

your umbrella bobs to the beat, kick it up Aunt Lavinia,
naughty & ninety, in your bright red hair

"You're doing a great job, Brownie," Bush sd on tv
to the pathetic FEMA director, a friend of a friend
of a friend, needed a job after the Arabian Horse Association
gave him the gate, couldn't manage horse shows —
"You're doing a great job Brownie,"
white men congratulate each other
& smile, cruelly clueless, they are the disaster

Mama Bush sd she thought the refuges at the Houston Astrodome
never had it so good — "this is a good situation for them.
many of them were disadvantaged you know."
Mama Bush went back to one of her mansions.
we went back to Section 347, near the end zone,
& got ready to line up for bottled water

Voodoo Queen Marie Leveau floats in the mist
around her sepulcher
in St. Louis # 1 — her white stone adorned
with a worse for wear wreath,
red streaks, etched names, water lapping its base —
sirens moaned somewhere, or was it a distant, angry wind?
the mist shifted, twisted like a dancer, or a rope
pulled through itself, & with it, the wispy form vanished

Doubloons of Jean LaFitte blizzard from the floral
pirate floats, the Mississippi swallows the streetcar named Desire,
Lake Ponchatrain demands its piece of southern pecan pie,
we're second lining sloshily through the streets for the dead,
our umbrellas bob & weave between the rain drops,
the music of death can only be the music of life
& the French Quarter will never die

On Blue Monday they reported Fats Domino among the missing —
he was a proud man, they all sd, & he loved his city —
didn't want to go nowhere — he'd found his thrill,
his Blueberry Hill

pounding the piano, grinning — only one Fats Domino —
a Cheshire Cat smile on the American brain —
Fats bobbed up safe on . . . *Saturday morning, o Saturday morning*

Gris gris on the bayou
Dr John fingers on the pulse
of Satchmo's foghorn
Buddy Bolden stirs the cauldron
Big Chief Jolly & the Wild Tchoupitoulas Indians
beat the nouveau tom-tom
runaway slaves & renegade Creeks
create a new tribe, a new band.

Andrew Jackson wades through the swamp
in his crooked Napoleonic hat, he pursues
Indians, alligators, a political future, New Orleans
the prize that will open all doors, even the French ones
in the White House, but no one can possess New Orleans,
Jackson has come & gone, but Osceola remains in the swamps.

The dancers held their umbrellas to the sky
dipping & bopping
as the rains fell
& the wind blew plaintively,
but soon it was time to get out of the storm,
& after a while we wondered if we would ever get out of the storm

Lee Harvey Oswald passed out pro-Commie leaflets
to establish a pre-assassination identity, & upstairs
Bannister & Ferrie plotted & chanted private eye spells,
Ferrie did bizarre experiments with mice — some kind of CIA
Voodoo potion — Carlos Marcello called a lot of shots down here —
Clay Shaw was slick — Alligator eyes peer over the water

Don't call me a refugee,
I'm an American!
they stood on their little piece of shore
& watched my city drown.
they congratulated themselves

as I clung to the roof of my house.

Here by the banks of the bloody Mississippi
was where they sold live human flesh.
They didn't exactly see them as people.
These were economic transactions.
Now slavery's abolished.. But money still rules.
After the levees broke,
they didn't exactly see them as people.

Blow, Golden Sax man! Fill it, Mr. Bass.
O Clarified Clarinet, you & Your Highness
Sir Trumpet rule this parish,
soar above earthen Time
O Pulse of Drum, make that shifting beat
polyrhythmic, seismic, awaken & transform
this nation's consciousness

BLOW BIG MAN

photo of David Hines blowing his horn:
belly & wrists protruding, as if bursting
out of his suit, right hand
holding trumpet, fingering valves,
mustached lips pursed, cheeks puffed, eyes
focused behind tinted shades,
left hand outstretched
leading the band

now in heaven
a spirit

Miles hangs on my wall
as well,
torn from a newspaper,
leaning back & leaning in

& Coltrane's up there too
as Roy DeCarava caught him
pouring light

They be blowing
their brains out
hovering over
my writing desk

We all just hanging here
in my basement
listening

Blow, they say,
silently,
blow Big Man,
blow

DON CHERRY LIVE

Don Cherry chants in Sanskrit,
Chants Japanese, chants African tongues.
Don Cherry does finger mudras,
steeples, knots, turns hands
inside out to palms up,
infinite giving gesture, invites
"try it."
Don Cherry strums *duzongoni*,
the hunter's guitar,
& hums.
Don Cherry's voice
trills like a bird.
Don Cherry blows
his pocket trumpet.
Sits on floor & tinkles
on a tiny piano.
Don Cherry works out
a new mind mantra—AAAAH.
Don Cherry's lighter than air.
Don Cherry's got hollow cheeks.
Don Cherry smiles
& light pours from his eyes.
Don Cherry gives us a chant
& improvises over it.
Don Cherry gives us the clap—
"You clap on the one
& you give on the four."
We make music
chanting & keeping beat
with Don Cherry.
Don Cherry blows over
us, trumpet in one hand,
orchestrating with the other.
Don Cherry accepts a white rose
& a red one, & a woman's smile

& starts chanting.

Don Cherry ends in mid phrase, saying
"Maybe we should all go out
& look at the moon."

BLUES FOR THE MUSE

O Muse, thou givest me
the Blues
I ope' my door to let you in
my empty room
& you send chilling breezes
in yr stead
that ache my knees
& shake my head
with images of gloom & doom

O Muse, thou givest me the blues
Yr absence takes my breath away
leaving nothing to inspire
My pen is for your hire
I offer you my golden soul
Yet you play hard to get
A wet
blanket for my smoldering fire
A shovel for my hole

O Muse, thou givest me
the Blues
The page weeps in white silence
The computer screen sobs all blank & blue
like my mind, left darkened by yr absence
You do me violence, sad but true
without yr pacific oceanic touch,
the waves of words don't flow
A constant ebbing marks me now
Limp, I need your crutch

O Muse, thou givest me
the Blues
But maybe i'll just take 'em
& make 'em mine
& etch a song to mark a stark dark time
of abandonment & not abandon

Then at least i'll keep my hand in
motion with emotion, stir up some dark potion
whose rank smell will twitch yr nose
with pangs of curiosity that say,
don't blow, go see
& bring you back to me

O Muse, thou givest me
the Blues
& so I thank you with a curse
Blank Bitch, it could be worse
The Blues was good enough for Lightnin'
Leadbelly, Muddy, Blind Boy & the rest
Maybe it's your flipside, Muse, your shiny head's
dull blurry tail,
your sunrise setting in the west
Still lover of your light, I vow now not to fail,
but to wail, & accept your test.

◆

O Muse, thou givest me the Blues

HORN OF PLENTY
for Maurice Malik King (1943-1994)

1.

Malik lays on the hospital bed, unconscious,
hooked to machines monitoring every bodily function,
comatose, breathing heavily, responsive
only to pinpricks, not to words.
We talk to him. Maybe he hears.
We tell him those things we don't normally.
How much we love him. How he is us.
We remember his vitality, his joy in living,
the beautiful music of his soul and gleaming
saxophone & eyes.
I don't want to remember him this way,
bloated, near naked, splotched with sores. I remember
the way he said my name,
the lift it always gave. Brother Malik,
if I could lift you now
out of this limbo,
out of this bed, out of this room & its white gloom,
I would. I would lift you gently,
like the notes of a golden horn
blown by the purest of breaths.

2.

One of the songs we blew
that spoke especially to you
described climbing a mountain
in a blinding blizzard, seeking to see
the other side —
the *unmapped territory* —
you went there with your horn of plenty
each time you picked it up —
you're there now brother —
the other side of the mountain high
is unmapped territory.

3.

What did you play?
"Time & Condition," you'd say,
shaking your head.
"Time & Condition ..."
Your tone poem
blown fresh every set,
nourishing as bread
straight out of the oven—

How ya doin'?
"Cake's all Dough," you said.

AUGUST 1982: MISSOURI
& America Lose Three Poets to Death
for Tom McAfee, Mbembe Milton Smith
& Arthur Brown

3 MISSOURI POETS DEAD!

    headlines don't read

    A profound silence
    aches the head
    attacks the heart
    of America—Columbia,
    Kansas City, St. Louis
    highland, plain, & river
    towns hoarse with grief,
    flowers wilting in the heat,
    hearses drift down sleepy downtown streets
    voices gone downstream
    unheard beneath the river murmur
    of blood & bones, roots & earth

    These dog-days leave us panting,
    chanting ancient prayers, public
    praise songs & private curses,
    wiped out & weeping,
    sweating & sleeping,
    huddled together silent
    & disbelieving, gently reaching
    out hesitant fingers to touch
    each other's still
    live damp flesh

    The death of a poet
    is a terrible thing,
    & three of our tribe have gone
    these dog-days
    answering cries of the lost
            guide Cerburus,

tuned to dark barks
we can't quite
hear
draw
near

O cities of the heart
enduring your dull, dumb, pain
· with dazed expression
News sheets cover your poets,
bury them on back pages,
noticing death in tiny type

Reporters who ignored
sit bored at "hearings" & don't attend
spirits' fluted whispers or saxophone shrieks
More important stories
out there, they dream,
than the cool facts
of life & death laid out here

OBITUARILY

the poets' language,
spirit,
consciousness
that touched us

untouched

      the dream,
the press
of who we are,
were, can be
that Tom, Mbembe, Arthur released

mappers of this territory:
highland, plain, & river

unaddressed,
        uncaressed
  suppressed
    depressed

valleys of America
yawned
as wispy McAfee smoked
in his wasting cancer
& spoke the intense spaces
between you & me;

& Mbembe opened the window
to let in light
of a clear mean broken bottle of a day
down on the corner
then leaped;

& Arthur scribed & sung his river
song & oceanic vision
then suddenly drowned in the flood
of a fluttering heart

Who would not sing for these who
themselves sang
deeply the bittersweet
poetics of life, the treasured curse
of our space, our place, our
multi-uni-verse

Who would not sing, indeed
for the poets
        who sang for us
these dog days under the hot sun

We ache for our friends,
our vigorous & strong voices,
for the music unheard
  on the radio,

the news not noted
   in the papers,
the images unresolved
   on the tv

we ache for the void inside us

Three of our tribe are gone
these dog days
Three voices
         still

      in mind

THE LONELINESS & GENEROSITY OF THE WORD
for Robert Creeley (1926-2005)

painful
to watch,
hear,

in the 9am modern
poetry class,
you struggling

to find the right

word, right
phrase, *that is,*
you spoke,
haltingly, *i.e.*

in short bursts,
inhaled back,
& tried again,

two steps
forward, one . . .
like they say,
you'd say,

grimace,
narrow
yr good right eye,
as if to see more

clearly, *i mean,*
clearly enough to
satisfy

yr good ear

POET IN A TREE
for Gabor G. Gyukics

prune it down
to focus the energy

don't be afraid
to go out on a limb

HOW THINGS STACK UP
for Chaitanya Vyas

I stack my American coins in neat piles
on the table before me:
quarters the foundational bottom,
followed by nickels, pennies, dimes.
A mini-tower of mini-money.
I leave my room for the Indian world
where the rupee is the language
of commerce, not value.
Value is smiles, family, friends, all
by the grace of God.

A quick exchange with Chaitanya:
"I have seen people go
from Heaven to Hell in a second,"
he says. Then, "Forget 'if,'
eliminate 'if' from your vocabulary,"
says, "you can't live
in the past or in the future.
Now's the only time. Tomorrow
it could all be dust. . ."
waving his hand,
"Enough of philosophy,"
& stalks off.

I go upstairs, sit down,
brush the table with my foot.
The tower of coins,
so painstakingly erected,
tumbles, & clatters to the ground
in all directions.

BASEBALL
for Danny Spell

holy
cow — he
dropped the pop-
up   me
first chance at
first base

i could've
died

spit

in yr glove
sd the ump
to the distraught
ten yearolder

& so (sigh)
i did & i
rubbed the bubbly saliva in
with my bare hand

baseball can teach you
(nothing
       but)
           patience

sipping cigarettes, grandmas
sewing moebius seams
round horse's hide

     hide

you'd like to but you can't
so squint in the face

the glaring err-
     roar

swaying on the sultry
porch, a rocker
& a radio, breezy,
keeping track

2 & 2
becomes 3
& 2, something
gives

i marched down broadway
with the St. Jude's Comets
in the opening day parade,
circa
          1957, Dyckman Little League,
181st St to 207th,
Inwood park, the Big Apple--
struck out then
hit a homer
off the flame-throwing lefty, Billy Guinon,
of the Good Shepherd Shamrocks,
line drive down the line. . .
          opposite field. . .
          the crowd rising
          in my mind
touch 'em all
itchy flannel uniform I
                    loved
          holy
                    green stained knees
wearing
                    number 37

the glory
that was Roma's

Pizza, the hurler,
like some heroic warrior
embronzend at the center
of a vast sundrenched
arena

the batter waving
a menacing wand

the deliberate
motion
slow   as   summer

pissy beer
          flattening
                    in the sun

the minds

of all the players
coaches, umps
all the fans

poised together

the ball
                    all
the world

hard
          to make good contact with
consistently

30 percent success
considered excellent, not including
fouls, & other empty
strikes

a certain

mostly silent music
      a rhythm

the coaches' signs

the crack
    the thump
        the count

comments from the peanut gallery
      we're talking
facts
      & figures, relationships, statistics, history

      swings

      missed

           opportunities
    dreams

wind-ups
& deliveries

connections,

moments
of truth,
when everything coheres:

mind & matter
motion & emotion

stan the man &
nature

    of reality

      in the floating

world

slider
curveball
knuckler
screwball
duster
smoke

SHEKINA

She rose, a creature of light,
a lily, rising in her dewy bed, stretched
her body of light & 13 rays shot out,
13 rays of consciousness materialized in the void
between sleeping & waking,
she rose & wrapped herself in 13 petals,
a Lily of the West, rising in morning's eastern light
above the saloon, rose to dance in the warm wind
of barroom bluster below, a dance hall gal,
a Lily, a flower among the thorns
in the Wild West of Creation.

◆

O the rednecks & roughnecks & rubber necks
that clattered through the swinging doors!
How they whistled & stomped & brawled & bled
for beauty & booze. How they cut
the decks of destiny
with dung-flecked fingers & gun-greased hands
how they reached out to pluck every fruit & flower
wavering before them in the bloodshot smoky light.

O how Lily danced!
O how her 13 leaves, her 13 feathered fans, rose
& fell, revealing & concealing her loveliness &
luminous core. How she engulfed the mind &
soul as she
tantalized, & eluded their grasp. How her hair
flamed red as fire,
how she flared off warmth & glow,
& could not be held in hands or arms or mind.

O Lily of the West. I conceive your memory.
I saw you dance
on the sawdust stage of the Golden Slipper.

I was among the rollicking miners
who lay bags of treasure
alongside the footlights,
who showered you with powdered gold.
O you were powerful & radiant.
I saw your eye-beam humble a heckler,
your darting glance make a groper grovel,
your flash of disdain straighten up a crook.

O Lily, Lily. O holy flower, wholly
out of reach. How you stripped each petal
& glided with amazing grace in the soft eye of spot,
how you teased us, bumping & grinding down
to your bare essentials,
how when the thirteenth feather floated
into the gaping pit of the awed orchestra,
it revealed you

gone.
Just traces
of your movements
etched in the light

that darkening morn.

AUGURIES OF EXPERIENCE

When man aspired
down he fell
losing Eden
finding Hell

Earth became
a suffering place
a path to death
the human race

& death meant fear
& awe & doubt
God cast aspiring
angels out

of Heaven
where He lived alone
contemplating
what He'd done

Love still lived
amidst the strife
Man took Woman
for a wife

In time
they struggled to be free
to use the knowledge
from the tree

But knowledge proved
a clever cage
mankind rattled
mad with rage

God just frowned
& tipped the pole
Darkness fell
on every soul

BITTER PENANCE

Eating the apple might have been a mistake.
We bit off more than we can chew.
I wish I could spit it out

in Your Face

but, unfortunately,
it's stuck in my craw.

SATORI IN BUDAPEST

On the plain of Pest,
as I entered
the Dohany Street Synogogue,
the second largest in the world,
they cautioned me,
Keep Your Hat On.

& in Buda,
up on Castle Hill,
in Mathias Church,
named after the first nation builder,
I was chided:
Take Your Hat Off.

Confused,
I went to my friend, Gabor,
for advice.
"It's the same God,
isn't it?" I moaned.
"What does he want?
"Who's lying?"

"Both,"
he said.

◆

Then he looked at me
& smiled &
I understood —

poets are pagans.

ESCAPE TO PARADISE
a ghazal sandwich for Ed Boccia

I.

The exploding fish cigar's smoke is a bother
Makes it feel like the party's over. . . *wondering what comes next.*

Saggy, weary, alone together
Was I ever really your lover? . . *wondering what comes next.*

O yes, you chased me in my youth,
When I was quite the mover. . . *wondering what comes next.*

Days of splendor, clear blue skies,
Hard now to recover. . . *wondering what comes next.*

The time of the serpent is at hand.
Its bite stings like a mother. . . *wondering what comes next.*

A walking fish, a crucifix,
The snake has shed his cover. . *wondering what comes next.*

I'll leave my skin to all my kin
To fight over with one another. . . *wondering what comes next.*

Where do we go when the lights go low,
Can you tell me brother? . . *wondering what comes next.*

I'm stranded on this sandy shore;
Is that you on the other. . . *wondering what comes next.*

II.

Idly viewing the water
We know the nature of things —

Looking away, the mind spins.
The whirlpool world sucks me down.

196

Paradise a good cigar to savor
till the moment it explodes,
& I drown in a rain of ashes.
Life has caught me with my pants down.
Slither around me. If the asp bites, let it.
The serpent is always at hand.
The apple dangling.
The hanged man.

Why did we ever leave the sea?
Crucify me with the fishes.
An I for an eye. A me for a we.
Idly viewing the water . . .

Alone together, a private island.
Every I-land bounded by a boundless sea.
But our vision is limited.
We can't see beyond the horizon.
We can't even see our true selves clearly.
Breathing clouds the mirror.
Trapped in seedy bodies,
Love explodes with flashes of light
we become.
We bask in it, fading, a comforting afterglow,
a sunset. Selfless eyes —

Idly viewing the water, we know the nature of things.

III.

I remember vowing, *Paradise or Die!*
You led me to your garden on the sly. . . *& we were lovers*

In a strange light time stood still,
The bee nuzzled the flower's petal cup & drank it dry
. . . *sated lovers*

The bee taught the flower to buzz,
The flower taught the bee to sigh. . . *learning lovers*

Two became one, the world one too,
The shore & the sea, the sea & the sky. . . *transcendent lovers*

We dreamed paradise in moments outside time.
And were pelted by alarm clocks by and by. . . *awakened lovers*

Two little people in one big world,
Plummeting so low, after soaring so high. . . *deep diving lovers*

Paradise like a palmful of ocean,
flows through our fingers in the blink of an eye. . . *clinging lovers*

Your song's an escape to Paradise, Castro,
or maybe just a plaintive cry. . . *for all lovers*

MR. PRYSTOWSKI

Mr Prystowski
taught us Bible in Sunday School
at Beth Am, The People's Temple.
He was younger, more attractive
than the other (all male) teachers:
Mr Bernstein, sweat glistening over his lips,
broadcasting the indecipherable Hebrew lessons
with shifting eyes,
desperate for the attention of spitball rolling
twelve year olds
yet he taught me, in his junior high gig, first
shakespeare,
romeo & juliet, as you like it,
especially the all the world's a stage speech

& half-bemused, half-disgusted Mr. Riisman,
solving the problem of getting through the hour
of "Guidance" by making us write uncollected
unfinished essays: copy the text if you like--
as a way to pass the time.
He'd read the newspaper.

But Mr Prystowski held us wrapped in his delivery
challenged us with questions, seduced us
with his youth, his good looks, overcame the barrier
of his nerdy first name, Seymour, going by
the ultra-cool Sy. Mr Prystowski
taught us the *Book of Job*,
explored the deal between God & Satan
to test a man's faith, to torture someone,
to make a good man suffer
loss of wealth, loss of children,
a body burning with boils, Mr. Prystowski,
Sy, describes each catastrophe. How could Job
not cry out in his misery? he demands.
How could he not descry his God?

Or when the three friends come & offer comfort
& advice--don't blame God they say—
how their words ring hollow, Mr. Prystowski says.
"I am guiltless, free of transgression," Job insists.
"I am innocent, without iniquity," Job protests
(too much for God),
but he's right, Mr. Prystowski says.

O Kafka! O Josef K! O Jews
rejecting & projecting guilt with every breath,
feeling sorry for ourselves saddled with our raw deal
tough-love, uncommunicative Father!

God
speaks to Job though, boasts really, about His power,
echoes
the arguments of Job's three friends
indignantly—question Me!
(& then throws some suffering their way
because even they weren't sincere enough for Him).
You can't win.

Josef K. lies on a slab in the quarry,
like Isaac; the knife passes over him.

Job, cowed by God's words, intimidated, Mr.
Prystowski says,
by a vision of His awesome power, pledges his love
in terror.
Overwhelmed, terrified, realizing
his own insignificance,
Job becomes the exemplary devotee once again,
& his health & wealth are restored.
(*But what about the dead children??!*, the question),
the question, Mr. Prystowski points out, lingers:
Life *is* unfair.

"One man dies in robust health
All tranquil & untroubled;

His pails are full of milk;
Another dies embittered,
Never having tasted happiness.
They both lie in the dust
And are covered with worms."

Why do good people suffer
while bad ones prosper?
Where is justice?
Mr. Prystowski implores,

hands outstretched, face pained, demands we
consider the questions, the answer. "The answer,"

he says, "is
there is no answer."

"The answer is there is no answer."

What a thing for a twelve year old to ponder.

How could there be no answer?
O Mr. Prystowski, say it isn't so!
But Mr. Prystowski repeats, shaking his head:
"The answer is there is no answer."

*K. finds the air rarefied, stifling,
in the attics of The Law.*

We leave class puzzled & disappointed
to be left

hanging
beneath the tree of knowledge.

The answer is there is no answer.
The only lesson I remember from my Sunday School
daze.

LA AMERICA

(for Moise Gadol, editor & publisher of La America,
*   the first Judeo-Spanish language newspaper in*
the United States, 1910-1925)

Warrior for truth,
armed only with pen,
press, & knowledge
that language is power
the powerless don't know
they possess. *La America,*
your organ, vital
beat of a community body
politic, split into clans
Salonika, Rhodes, Monastir,
Constantinople, Kastoria, Adrianople,
Janina, Corfu,
the Lower East Side, Harlem, *La America*
    feeds all branches, nurtures
common root, transplants
ancient strength of language tree
to immigrant sidewalks,
                              dreams.

    Moses
of the ghetto, tablets
in your pockets, your jobs
are countless, hours endless;
    poverty is
                              timeless.

In the beginning
was the Word, Moise. & in *La America*
you we begin again. Touch
each new arrival, every
neighborhood group. Watch

your watch, pause, think, drink
coffee, eat okra at a cheap cafe;

plot, scheme
how to pay the bills; write
                notes:
this lunch
is research, remember
to mention the need for better food
in these Turkish corner joints in the next edition
(if you can get it out).

Then off to the next meeting, the next
argument, battle. Abuse & ridicule
your thanks. Bulgarians talk funny
they say. No matter.
Sephardim (believe you me)
    are clannish, proud
with good reason — *write*
    ignorance, provinciality
        the enemy; *write* poverty (a state
                        of mind), *write*
                            ego,
                    selfishness, stages
overcome — stress
through Unity. *Unidad. La*
  America, your organ, plays this song's
                        vital beat
                        over & over & over:

  Unity is Power.
Language is
    consciousness:

        the media
                the message.

            (Write
on, Ghetto Moe.
Don't mince
words.

203

Remind us
    of Babel. Demand
respect, reject
charity, speak out
offensively, x
    centrically — know God
is one, too; in exile,
too.)

Dead
                    in 1941,
Hitler stalking kin,
broke, half-nuts, buried
by your rival, who could not arrange
a grave site next to your wife's, or
even among our people.
Unity is Power. Is

anybody listening?
reading?
  praying?

You are remembered, Moise,
by a few, with wry smiles,
as that *original*
                    that
loco-meshugge

who claimed Christobal Colon was

one of us, hustling,
not knuckling under,
                            discovering
yet another home,
                    unfolding

    La America.

BAKSHEESH

Old lady beggar at the Shiva temple gate,
body an accordion of wrinkles,
mouth a toothless flap, making
moaning music —

bak
      sheesh,
bak
      sheesh,

sad solo song of the current Kali Yuga

thin palsied hand vibrating
atremble to her mantra's drone,
worn thin coins jangling
in an ancient iron cup

TYRANT:
Execution of Romania's Ceaucescu

I am dead.
I am full of holes.
I lie in my own blood.
I don't breathe.
I generate
death. Death
consumes me.
I lie among my lies.
My image, on
thousands of walls,
desecrated, torn down.

Who loved me?

So many volunteered
for the firing squad
Christmas day,
they held a raffle
& the winners joyously fired.
Flies graze on my wounds.
Soon I'll be dumped in a hole.
Unceremoniously.
To live among worms.

"No matter how much you feed them
the worms are always hungry,"

Elena said. But she was
speaking of the people.
And we laughed, and gave the orders.
Former, carefree times.

Elena's dead too. Beyond
reach. Soon
they'll plow us under.
Even now I see no light.

I can hear their cheers,
Different now,
more sincere.
My soul aches.
I can't rise.
I'm dead.

◆

I'll haunt them

UNDERGROWTH
after the Shoah

Train tracks overgrown with wild grass.
Roads to death overgrown with life.
Insistent life asserts identity
pushily, through the earth, needing

no classification, no numeration, no objectifying.
Whitman saw the grass's meaning
as "there is no death"
in absolute terms; & maybe
he's right, in absolute terms,
but here, by these tracks,
we deal with relatives.

Memory likes the grass to grow
likes the new to blur, & cover, & bury,
prefers the smell of dewy grass & spring's promises
to that of mass graves at the end of the line.

& so we survive, overgrowing, overgrown,
pushing forward life
& would, if we could, ignore
who we are
in a deep & rooted sense,
letting life's grassy fragrances
prevail.
But we can't quite forget.

The anguished ghosts are sometimes insistent
as the grass covering the tracks; haunting,
like mist over the field,
or a veil-like aura around us,

around the death trains' destinations,
places in Europe,
& in us.

The whispers of the ghosts are persistent, pushy,
they make us uncomfortable, for they are sounds of those
whose tongues were severed from the world,
whose names were denied,
whose souls & divinity
brutalized, unrecognized
& they whisper horrors,
in a soundless language,
of what was done to them,
of what can be done to us too,
for we bear
their imprint,
their names,
their blood
We too
are pushy with life.

And these voices within us
whisper & warn,
if you really listen,
in the pride of your identity,
in the pride of your assumed victimhood,
they tell of what you can become
on either side
of the awful human equation.

Enough of that.
We don't want to hear it.

But dealing with absolute facts,
relatively,

there are almost no Jews left living
in Greece now, where once, vaguely within memory,
there were many.
Silent voices,
speaking ghostly Ladino,
swell with the wind,

from time to time,
in Salonika, Jannina, Corfu.
The temples are desolate, decaying,
awesomely silent,
scrawled & slurred with graffiti.

And the tracks that
the people
men, women, children,
they *were* people,
humans,
rode away on,
packed like freight,
the tracks
are covered with wild grass
a dark wind whispers through.

The wind moves
pushily
through the high grass
of the graves of Europe.

HALLOWEEN

Today all the hungry ghosts
wail all the world's sorry chains
creak all its light leaks
into the dark
where hidden horror lurks

It's Halloween!
gargoyley guys
& shrewy witches
the underside
is the scratch we itches

A parade, in masquerade,
of tiny boys & girls, wide open
bags & palms, stream through seedy suburbs'
leaf-mealed lawns

innocents
trickling trick-less

stifling yawns

gathering more & more
door to door treats
from shadowed neighbors' smiles
sweets & coins
dispensed straight up or
with weird & twisted, hidden wiles

cold cash &
bidden fruit they there-
fore dare not grasp or eat
without exploratory
pause

preferably

laboratory
analysis

Once home
they sift through eager fingers
offerings that they sought, & brought

mull possibilities
laced treats & hot pennies
strained food for thought

& later bodiless, near
nauseous, overwrought,
they wrestle in the bed

wispy demons of the mind

reflections of this bitter world of humankind
whose cool coin's, glad hands' & twisted smiles'
impacts instead
may burn, or sicken, or, finally

kill you dead

TRICK OR TREAT
for Ira Cohen (1935-2011)

Horny rabbit hidden under your Hasidic fedora
Bickering doves rustling in your beard
Wilting bouquets swelling the folds of your black cloak
Magician, Wizard of Tangiers, Sage of Kathmandu,
You were he ultimate poetry trickster

Majoun Coyote, Panama Red, Akashic Recorder,
Mylar Mirror Man, Hunter & Gatherer
of sparks amidst the shards —
Hendrix in the fun-house, masked poets,
a toothless man with a skull in his hand

Every image you created,
every word you wrote, was the truth, you warned us,
surreal as it might be — the morning headlines
printed on cat fur, postcard satoris,
Paul Celan books under your Afghan hat,
outwitting the Labyrinth's security system forever —

You subverted capitalism with slight of hand
You snapped your fingers & tweaked the mind with pictures
You invited us to a Tokyo birdhouse to drink Tokay perhaps
to fly, or at least be tickled by the feathers —
insisting on Paradise Now.

& in the final act,
you're standing on the window ledge, wings clipped,
poems & other sacred objects – *"your shit"* they called it —
warehoused in a locker in New Jersey —
"My shit?????" "My Life!!!!!" you roared,
threatening to plunge
Dragged down by bedbugs & hospitals & samsara.

Now you bathe in the sacred underground river beneath Hardwar,
You & the other Holy Men in the ultimate *Kumbh Mehla*
Immersed in the goddess

213

& yet,
You & Mr. Natural were spotted sitting on a bench
on a traffic island on the Upper West Side .
Your spirit is walking the page on feet of gold.
Your eye is laughing in photographs, the moving
still pictures of eternity you directed,
starring your many friends —

Sorcerer of sneezes, conjuror of treats,
You performed the ultimate trick:
You're gone but still here in the Living Theater.

BY THE DANUBE

For Attila Jozsef & Gabor G. Gyukics

meditation by the statue of Attilla Jozsef
on the banks of the Danube
at the northern end of Budapest's corso,
no identifying signs around because no need,
everyone recognizes the mustachioed poet
sitting on humble wooden steps,
leaned over, hands dangling over knees,
intensely surveying the passing flow,
his cloak tossed off beside him,
statue flaking & cracked,
this is how he appeared
when he wrote "By the Danube,"
before he dove under a train,
this is where he watched an orange peel float by,
where he saw past, present & future
in the waves, where all Hungarians,
all humanity going back to the primordial cell
spoke through him, where he became
the Universal One,
& told everyone
to get it together —
"By the Danube"
Gabor & I, his translators,
sit at his feet —
the Danube flows by timelessly

PATCH OF LIGHT

In town for Adam's wedding on a grey weekend.
Time to kill in Columbus, where there is no sun,
except in Hopper's painting
in the museum I walk to in the rain.

It's stare there
or stare at factory rooftops & blank-eyed
office buildings out my hotel window. I stare
instead, timelessly it seems, at Hopper's painting
at the woman sitting up on her bed,
hugging her knees,
her nightgown pulled up around her waist.

She is staring out *her* window,
blank eyed, alone.
Nothing to see
but factory rooftops across the way,
their empty walls, empty windows,
the bare walls inside her room,
& whatever's inside her head,
or mine, as she looks out,
inside, at me.

In the dim gallery, I can hear the roar
of torrential rain outside, but
the room
in the painting
is bright, seeming to light up
the corner of the museum
with its bleak scene.

In the painting,
the naked wall behind
the near naked woman
in the barren room
is illuminated by a patch of sun.

The patch nearly covers the entire wall.
It mirrors the shadowy shape of a framed window,
a window that is so important
in this Hopper painting,
itself a window
I look through.

I stare fully at
the woman's empty stare,
her timeless glaze
connecting with my own,
drinking in her light,
as the rain beats relentlessly outside.

I wind up walking through a downpour
carrying her impressed image, sitting in that room
on that sun-drenched bed,
inside me. Carry it to the edge
of my own bed.

It is spring, the wedding season has begun.

Back in the hotel room, with my wet clothes off,
I too am filled with naked desire.
Looking out the window at empty office buildings
& decrepit factories
as the Spring rain keeps up its patter,
I sit still, half-dressed, damp,
lifting my eyes like budding flowers,
as a patch of light can be discerned
breaking through the distant sky.

CALCUTTA

power outage
   at the College Street Coffee House —
      conversation still charged

JAIPUR JUNCTION

Dressed like a princess
she cleans her baby's bottom.

All around her, men lay stuporous
on the station platform;
announcements blare from the loudspeaker
in staticky Rajastani;
people drift by
in saris, dhotis, bowlers & bangles —
a signal bell is ringing somewhere

she ignores it all, focused, absorbed
between her baby's bum,
in love's silent, solemn ceremony.

Husband kneeling by her side
dressed in white,
Hierophant to her Priestess,
pouring oblations of sacred water
over her fervent hand.

The water keeps flowing
The golden urn he tips in his hand
seems bottomless.

She digs deeply
between baby's rump cheeks' crack.

The infant boy is serene,
his eyes dreamy.

The day is warm.
Smoke from a portable stove is rising.
Under the steady stream of water,
baby's brown liquid turds trickle & ooze
through her jeweled fingers
onto the tracks below.

OLD PHOTOS

My 79 year old mother sifts through old photos—
finds some from her trip to "the islands"
with her "friend," a "very nice man"—says
"These you wouldn't be interested in,"
gathers them together, gives me the others,
the piles from after she met my father—

something's reawakened in her,
the tender way she holds
those older photographs,
meaningful only to her

TARLOSAURUS AT P.S. 98

Michael Tarlow is talking about dinosaurs again.
He knows more about them than anyone
in the sixth grade.
Mr Kaufman calls him Tarlosaurus Rex,
or Rex for short.
Michael Tarlow & Milton Jupiter
are always getting into trouble.
They like to sit together & giggle & shout out wisecracks.
Mr. Kaufman. separated them,
putting one in the first seat in the first row
& the other in the last seat in the last row.
Now they shout more than they used to whisper.
They are unstoppable.
Milton Jupiter is the best punch-ball player in the sixth grade.
He is the only boy with a girlfriend.
He is tall & handsome & tells everyone
Jupiter is the God of Thunder.
Sometimes the Catholic kids argue with him
& occasionally the Jews.
Each thinks there is no other god than theirs.
I'm willing to let him steal their thunder,
as Mr Kaufman says,
'cause I know Milton Jupiter can beat me up.
Michael Tarlow claims dinosaurs were smarter than human beings
& maybe he is right.
I have seen skeletons of dinosaurs at
The Museum of Natural History.
I believe they would beat Milton Jupiter up,
probably eat him up,
if he tried anything with them.
I believe Michael Tarlow would like
to be a dinosaur & sit anywhere he wants.

BYE BYE BEARD, SO LONG STASH
for Jomo

My face now naked as when I was born.

I peer into the mirror at this strange stranger. . .

Have I uncovered myself?
I stare long, hard,
turn, turn back again
who *is* that unmasked man?

Good gray poet gone,
head compressed, chin receded,
nose enlarged, an ordinary
guy—cut, shaved
by his own son
like poor dead Kronos—revealed, exposed
as less than what he seemed.
In this act, the son proclaims
his manhood.
Father shorn, bared
of bearded illusions
of potency, no longer
leading man in legend of his own mind, more like
extra. . . good-bye
gray hairs
bye-bye beard
so long stash
no more long thoughtful tugs tender self caressings.
Only stubble dots my barren facial field.
Younger seeming, older feeling
unrecognizable
on my way to true who
is that fellow
invisibility—*ah*
oh, ugh, words fail, trail
off, who, whom, hum . . .

Son looks at my blankness,
fleshed face he's never seen
since plopped on planet,
some eighteen years.
He's been agitating for this day
since manhood at thirteen, came at me
in a moment of weakness, armed with shears.

Now he's unimpressed.

"Hmph, Dad," he says,
grow a goat."

FOR MORRIE CAMHI (1928-1999)

This is a poem for my cousin Morrie
who I didn't meet till I was 42,
yet who I felt I knew
my entire life.
The first thing we did upon meeting
(in California) was pitch pennies
because we both had grown up in New York
as streetwise kids
& this ritual made up for
all those years & all those miles
had kept us apart.

I loved Morrie like an older brother.
I loved his photography.
I loved the idea
of another artist in the family.
I loved how he insisted
on forming a relationship
with his subjects
before he'd photograph them,
how he could trick them
into being human
before the camera's
paralyzing eye.
He'd provoke a response,
push their buttons
before he'd push the camera's,
play stone dumb if he'd have to
to dissolve their stony stiffness.

I loved how we loved
good food together,
how his parties always had
such a fantastic cast of characters,
and always included
a magician & a fortune teller,

to remind us magic & prophecy
were alive in the world.

& I loved his hugs,
our special family embraces
with Adelia & Lynn,
our huddle
where the only play we called
was play itself.
I loved this man
who embraced so many,
who used every trick in the book
of the street: shock, shame,
laughter, sorrow
to lead you
to yourself.

He taught living fully
to the death, & dying
with dignity & grace,
affirming life & love
to his final breath.

GETTING IT TOGETHER

Here is my cock, a derbied gent,
   rising to the occasion
    of a lady in need.

Here is everything, love, seed
   I bury in the soil of your soul.

Here we rock together
       on waves we create creating us,
  waves in which we merge   emerge
       constantly changing, two and one.

 Here I am, naked before you,
   crying softly your name.

Here, my love, here
   the inseparable, unnamable, uncontainable,
   spilling up over onto your shore, seeping down
into your core

LOVE POEM '83

I reached out & touched you
with a poem, unaware
in my glory, my heightened con-
dition, spot-lit on stage,
When I finally came down
to pass as one
among the other mortals
you greeted me—hello, good-
bye, with a kiss, fleeting
on the lips.
It stayed with me
as you have, these years—
longer than I would have
thought possible.
Your kiss. Souls.
Touched. Touching.
A quick exchange
suddenly more.

& more.
I cannot shake you.
Wriggle as I will.
A fish unraveling
a line. . . a poem. . .
a kiss.
Lines
to tie a moment
into twin loops.
A bow.
        We weave through
one
        another—
& the knot
holds.

THE DAILY GRIND

Going to work day after day, waking up
to morning rituals, meditate,
feed the cats, make the coffee, clean the litter box, drink, think,
face the gray, hope for light — the article about the thirty-seven year
employee on the verge of retirement: Any memories stand out?
It all kind of blurs together — is this why we're here — a few sharp
memories of joy or despair, all else a muddle . . .

Belly rumbling the warmth of morning coffee, wife asleep upstairs,
Cats napping, I sing, softly
depressing keys — my mother would confront me
the same way my wife now does — draw me out of my silent shell
the way a blank page can —
this is what love wants, what the poem wants,
to draw us toward intimacy, open us, read us like a book
joining minds & souls — I never was a philosophical poet,
Always more visceral than intellectual, more sensual than concrete,
More musical than most, shaping breath to evaporative spirit —

I want you, your lips, your breasts, your central fire
Warm me, nourish me, caress me, enfold me,
The deeper I dive within, the more I long for release,
expression

TAKES

A Master on vibes,
Karl Berger sd:
"There are no mistakes.
You *follow*
your mistakes."

♦

Scolding Naropa poets,
Phil Whalen pounded his ample belly:
"It come from here, damn it!
Here! Here!"

♦

Robert Ferguson
responding to my comment,
"I really like your love poems,"
smiled, & drawled,
"All I write is love poems."

♦

Dahveed Nelson,
one of the Last Poets,
was laughing,
& when I asked him why
he just kept smiling
a kind of shit-eating grin,
& shrugged, & looked around, & sd,
"just the wonder of it all,
that's all"

EIGHTEEN TIMELESS MINUTES

that Ann happened to be scrambling by the crevasse
in the cliff at Pueblo Alto
on the day of the solstice

& that she happened to look in
through the slit in the cliff face
down through the earth

& that she happened to see the spiral petroglyph
that no other visitor or worker at the park
had up to then sighted,

& that she happened to glance in to the hidden room
at that precise time
during the quadrennial eighteen minute period

when the dagger of sunlight
bisects the spiral form
etched on the flat stone slab far back in time

& that she was the only person in the world
who could have realized & processed
that observed information
& obsessed on it & developed it & understood it

& shared it with everyone else in the world
to the degree that she did,
& that it seemed she had been called

by the light
for that purpose
the light admitted

by the boulders & rocks
placed so casually as to appear
randomly natural

by Anasazi, they say,
maybe means "old ones,"
no one remembers

the penetrant light
intersecting precisely
the stone slab's spiral's center

solstice & equinox —
'sun dagger'
they called it

marking time's sacrifice
on the sunshaft calendar,
the mysterious spiral

etched on the hidden flat stone slab
& those surface stones
placed above by "Chacoan Einsteins"

just so, to appear random,
casually admitting too
the shadow of the moon,

in its nineteen year cycle
round earth as it turns,
marking that journey

on the nineteen turns
of the spiral on the altar
strange unchanging changes

ethereal etchings on the slab that's
shaped like coiled snakes, snail shells & galaxies,
speaking a language of shadow & light

quadrennial sunshafts
piercing, dividing
solstice & equinox

moon shadow creeping
over the labyrinth
turn to turn year after year

round & round moving
further & further in
toward the center of the spiral

Ann noted it all & how
in the nineteenth year
when the moon was furthest from the earth,

its hemispheric shadow
bisected the spiral perfectly
& then Ann noticed

at the solstices that year
with moon & sun
in extreme relation to earth

moon at its furthest, sun its nearest
in the womb-like cleft in the cliff
moonshadow & sundagger

met
& were one
for eighteen timeless minutes

on the stone altar
at the center
of the spiral bed

◆

all this recorded
on page & on film
by Ann herself

awed & mystified

at time's dance &
its sacrifice

this ritual language
of earth & universe,
of love & light & mind

THE GUIDE: MAIMONIDES' JOURNEY (2015)

THE GUIDE
For Moses Maimonides (1135-1204)

Moses ben Maimon,
Moses the Spaniard,
Moses the Jew,
Maimonodes, Moses
ben Maimon ha-Sepharadi,
The Rambam, giver
of the essence
of the law —
Mishnah Torah
gentle in manner, but fierce in in-
tellect, endurance, sheer nerve —
"from Moses to Moses,
there is no one like Moses:"

Cordoba 1135, Sepharad,
where this life begins,
amidst war & woe, caught
between one interpretation & the other

Allah, Allah,
the Alhmohades insist
on their version of the name
of God who is beyond
names (we say), they don't
listen, in the name of Allah,
the Almohades burn down
the corrupted Islamic mosques
of those whose accent's off;
we don't even speak
the same language;
& the synagogues burn too on general principles —
Jews must swear allegiance to Allah,
must pay lip service
& through the nose —

It's not the names we fear,

it's the sticks, the stones,
    the fire —
Amidst flames not of a burning bush —
but of burning books,
scorched scrolls, smoking letters,
my wanderings began —

pero
       ningun encarcelado, se puede descarcelar.

  (No one is a prisoner if he can escape.)

& so we left our home, our wealth

     si los anios calleron, los dedos quedaron

  (If the rings fell off, at least the fingers stayed)

we fled through Sepharad, from town to town, to Almeria.
the Almohades hot on our heels

Cominos macarones, alambicos corazones.

(We ate macaroni, & licked our hearts.)

& when the Almohedan armies stormed Almeria's gates,
we set sail for Africa, Morocco.
Thus began my journey: Fez, Acco, the Holy Land,
Alexandria, Cairo. *My mind was troubled,*
& amid divinely ordained exiles, on journeys by land
& tossed by tempests of the sea . . .

Sepharad was our Jerusalem, our jewel, a garden
we had tended, transplanted trees,
& put down roots. . .
we knew the bite
of the olive and the fig, the land's strange fruits
we tried to live
amidst the Christians, amidst the Muslims,

238

to work through our *tikkun* & now
another wound to heal . . . another burning
temple

I think of those round Andalusian hills,
  the play of God's light off the green leaves
after a cleansing rain
              as I watch

the gray waves
  rise & fall,
the horizon flat
 as unleavened bread.

    Quien no sabe de mar,
     no sabe de mal.

      (He who knows nothing of the sea,
   knows nothing of suffering.)

          ◆

Since we went into exile,
    the persecutions have not stopped.
I have known affliction since childhood,
    since the womb.

Ah, the sun, the beautiful sun
that creates this desert, the aching beauty
of these desert flowers. . .

The greater the pain,
 the greater the reward.

Fez is a labyrinth.
Everything is hidden: the faces of its women
behind dark veils, the sumptuous interiors
of its white-walled, shuttered homes
Here we hide in plain sight.
Tired of running.

The Almohades approach the city gates.
Some say, resist, refuse, martyr yourselves—
    as others have. But I say, be calm,
when the Almohedes come to your door,
listen carefully to their conditions—
    If they are as we hear,
submit &
take the vow.

    Before you protest,
think it through:
In the earlier religious persecutions
we were forced to violate certain *shalls* and *shall nots*
through our deeds. In the present persecution, however,
no deed is demanded of us,
only *words*. A *name*.

I am a man of words, but listen to me O Jews.
We do not need martyrs. Resist
the long winded foolish babbling & nonsense
of those who argue for unflinching death.
Use your heads.

 Live *your name*
behind closed doors; cover your windows.
After all, if someone wishes to observe
all 613 laws in private, no one hinders him.

Now, if they tried to force us to commit a forbidden act,
of course, we would rather be killed than carry it out.
But there has never been so strange a persecution
in which we are forced to transgress only verbally.

Lie then, & live
the truth.

    Submit, for now,

Faste a amigo con el huerco,
hasta ques pases el ponte.

(Befriend the hangman,
    till you are over the bridge.)

but remember:

 Quien muncho se aboca, el culo se le vee.

(He who bends down too low, exposes his rear end.)

       ◆

I was of "the exile of Jerusalem
that was in Sepharad," as the book of *Obadiah* describes us.
And now we were doubly exiled. We
who had lived in Sepharad
before the Visigoths & the Vandals invaded,
before the Christians or the Muslims
were conjured up by their prophets,
before the Almohades, who were Berbers from Morocco,
began their righteous pillage, we
who were part of the soil & soul of that place,
   who helped to make a Golden Age, we

abandoned our ancient villages & ourselves
to God's will, without any signs
save those of danger, took up the challenge
with Hope & Faith & if truth be told,
with fear
for ourselves & for those
who remained behind

I landed in Fez, in the heart
of the beast.

      ◆

My desire & my quest

241

was to know God
so far as this is possible for a human being.

I mastered first mathematics, then the natural sciences,
especially to familiarize myself with their patterns
& subtle perfections,
before I grappled with metaphysics. My brother,
David, sailed around the world buying & selling
to support my efforts. This was his way
of worship & of love, & I studied, & I taught, & wrote.

I wrote many books, among them the *Mishnah Torah:*
here I put into one book
the unraveled strands, the distilled opinions,
the essence of Talmudic wisdom.
Someone had to resolve the disputes, the split hairs,
the rabbinic quibbling, & testing —
Who could really read through the whole *megillah*
of the Talmud, that weighty treasure chest,
every time another dispute arose?
Here it is, I said, & people listened & read:
the naked heart
of the matter.

I wrote from mind, & breath, & source —
from God, seeking God.

My only master was Aristotle.
Reading him encouraged me to live
in the mind, showed me
that thinking is godly,
implying

that even a master, an Aristotle,
is not to be followed
blindly. Blind dedication,
blind faith, blind obedience
leads to blind fanaticism, blind persecution,
blind hatred.

What's a mind for, I thought,
    if not to help us
see?

      ♦

Some call me "Rabbi."

      ♦

I advise my neighbors & friends:
  never eat except when hungry, or drink except when thirsty.
      Observe moderation. Don't go out in the cold after bathing.
  Avoid constant bloodletting.

Be guided by *hesed*: lovingkindness & compassion;
        tsedekah: righteousness;
        mishpat: judgement.

     For stating the obvious,
        I am called wise.

Everyone wants to obey
    someone.

We are too immersed in tradition,
too bogged down in faith, too frozen
in ritual. In our exile
we have forgotten
  how to think.

   And therefore, we must train the mind,
 as we do the body:

Think of God
as a King.
& think
        how, in a kingdom,

some have more direct access than others.
In the Kingdom of God,
those who have studied
the mathematical sciences & logic,
& who have studied the Talmud,
but who have not asked
whether the propositions found there
are actually true, these seekers
wander around the walls of the palace,
looking in vain for the entrance.

And those who have studied the mathematical sciences & logic,
& who have studied the Talmud
& *the natural sciences*
& actually thought about them,
these seekers enter the palace's forecourt.

But those who have studied the mathematical sciences & logic,
who have studied the Talmud,
the natural sciences,
& *metaphysics*, & who have thought
about all of them,
    & understood what can be understood —
    these seekers arrive
    in the interior of the royal palace.

Thinking is a way to God.

   Consider this:
The prophet who "sees" God
does not really see in form
He who is beyond form.
The prophet is thinking
of God.

And when God is said to see
something, as He doesn't have sense organs, truly
He is contemplating the world.

God is a perfect intelligence.
The thinking that pours out from God
upon us is the link between Him & us.

We must solidify this link
& make it more intimate,
or it will gradually loosen
& dissolve altogether.

I am doctor, attending at the birth
& rebirth of philosophy, metaphysics,
imagination, & prophecy.
I labor at preparing the way
to the *Protecting King*, the *Active Intellect*.
I teach the burnishing & restoring,
the lighting of the inner lamp —
the bond of light between God & us —

The more active the mind,
 the more open to God.

For just as we know God by the light
that he has streaming out to us,
thus does He look through us
by means of this light.

This light is what makes everything
we see or do possible.

& yet this light is so brilliant
no one alive can
stare directly into it.

◆

There have been times when I have lost the light.
I dwelt in darkness
when my beloved brother, David, died at sea;
my world collapsed.
There were days I moaned in despair. What was the logic of the bad

happening to the good?
Why is it that each of us is Job?
How do we fill the loss of love?
My friends & family gathered & we wept.
We cursed & praised, we remembered, & we prayed.
We chanted *Kaddish*.
Its mystic sounds & rhythms
gave us a music to calm the soul.
We could not understand its ways & power,
or the ways & power of our God.
We pictured David in our minds, where he would always live.
Rains came, & we thought it was David, cleansing & renewing
            our shattered reality.
We felt his presence.
& the presence of God.

◆

I say to you, there is nothing
but God and His works. & His works include
everything in existence except God.
God is One: his own source
& the source of everything else.

God be thanked for all conditions,
whose universality is to be found
in the universe of existences
& whose specificity is to be found
in every single individual.
May the praise for every single condition
be constant, no matter what the situation may be.

◆

To support myself, & others,
I became a Doctor. For many years
I have worked
long hours to improve the human condition.

Now, even in my old age,
I go to Cairo every morning
at the crack of dawn to treat the Sultan
& his family, and if nothing unforeseen happens,
if nothing keeps me there, I can come home in the afternoon
but never earlier. Here, starving as I am,
I find the antechamber full of people: Jews
& non-Jews, nobles & lowly people, judges & officials,
friends & foes, a motley company awaiting me
with impatience. I dismount from my horse, wash,
& enter the waiting room with the plea that they
may not feel offended if I have to make them wait a bit longer
while I partake of a hasty light meal, which normally happens
once every twenty-four hours. Then I go out to them again,
treat them, & prescribe medicine on notes.
Thus the people go in & out of my home until late in the evening.
Sometimes, I swear on the Torah,
it is after midnight or even later
before I manage to consume anything.
I am then so worn out that I collapse on my bed;
I have to say good-night. I am totally exhausted
& incapable of speaking. Only on the Sabbath
can anyone speak to me alone, or can I be alone with myself,
if only for little more than an instant.
Then the members of my community
gather in my home after the morning prayer.
I indicate what is to be done in the community
during the coming week; then they listen to a lecture
until noon, go home, and return in smaller number
for another lecture. Thus do my days go by.

I teach & I heal. I give all I have
        to continue, to improve, to perfect
                the creation.
                        This is our purpose.
                        I think.

There are four perfections:

the perfection of wealth a king's perfection —
illusory because transient

the perfection of health the body's perfection —
important because a well-tuned instrument
keeps the mind clear;

But these things we look upon as the basis of happiness —
riches or health are not
the purpose of life.

There is the third perfection — perfection of character —
moral perfection, which contributes
to the social good.

This perfection improves mankind,
& provides important training for the mind;

for only a person whose character is pure, calm,
& steadfast can attain to the fourth —
intellectual perfection

the ability to acquire correct conceptions;
the perfection of the highest intellectual qualities;
training the mind to a rigor & openness
capable of receiving divinity;
capable of expanding to God.

◆

The Lord of the Universe
knows in what condition I write these lines.
I have withdrawn from people & sought peace
& quiet in order to remain undisturbed. At times,
I lean against the wall; at times, I continue my writing.
I am so feeble that I mostly have to lie down;
a weak body has joined forces with my age.

My body aches & breaks, but still I work, still
I study, still I think, still I try to heal & improve.
I observe, remember, make notes, logical connections.

But logic cannot tell us where creation comes from,
or why nothing leads to something. Knowing God
                is beyond thought, beyond words &
                                their source.
            How can you compare 100 cubits
                    to the sharpness of pepper?

        Know that there is a level that is higher
        than all thought, than all philosophy:
        Call it "prophecy."

        Prophecy is a different world.
        Arguing and investigating are out of place here;
        no evidence can reach prophecy;
                any attempt to examine it in a scholarly manner
                is doomed to fail. It would be like trying to gather
                all the water in the world in a single cup.

                            ◆

When the Bible says, "And God said,"
it means, "A Prophet understood."
God chooses prophets
from among those
whose minds are finely honed,
& whose imaginations
are vital: those who are open
to seeing new forms & combinations.

A prophet must be able
to actively think,
& then to rationally convey
& defend his experience.

Prophecy is not learning.
It breaks on you like a lightning storm.
It is like the weather.
The wisest man can go through life
and never experience the whirlwind.

◆

My whole life I have tried
to be a guide to the perplexed.

You have doubtless heard about the controversies I have had
against those who come before me with my tongue,
against those who attack from afar with my pen.
There was a time I would obtain satisfaction for myself
with my tongue and quill
even against the great & the wise
when they polemicized against me.
But now I know that pride & anger are very ugly qualities.

Then, if someone said I am neither pious nor religious,
it would infuriate me.
Now, I would not resent it--on the contrary
I would speak good gentle words to them, or hold my
tongue, depending on the circumstances. I seek no victory
for the honor of my soul; character
consists in deviating
from the paths of fools,
not in conquering them.
        If a man wanted to wax wroth
about the ignorance of men, he would never stop
being angry, & would lead a life of grief & affliction.

◆

Know then,
I have set myself the goal of behaving humbly
in every action, even though it damages me
in the eyes of the world.

If someone wishes to flaunt his own excellence
by demonstrating my failings, then I forgive him,
though he may be one of the most insignificant students.
Our leaders along the paths of good have said:
If one is to help both a friend and an enemy,
then one is required to help the enemy first
in order to subdue and to tame passions.
Anyone who wishes to be a human being
should work toward perfecting his character
& acquiring knowledge, he should not occupy his mind
with stupidities.

Remember, the necessary things are few in number.
while the superfluous things are unlimited.

◆

Thoughtfulness
outlives each
& all.

UNCOLLECTED & NEW POEMS (2015-2016)

WE NEED TO TALK

I am more than your idea,
I am tangible, touchable,
a human being like you.
We breathe the same air,
want the same things.
We need to talk.

I am more than my skin tone,
more than the weight I bear,
more than the clothes I wear,
more, even, than my hair,
more than who I sexually prefer,
more than my accented speech,
hear me! — we need to talk.

So get out of your closed mind,
It's claustrophobic in there — thoughts fester
if they can't expand. Let's meet.
Get out of your car, onto the street.
Let's discover each other
on common ground.
We need to talk.

I say, take off your armor,
put away your gun,
don't just stare dumbly into your
smart phone.
Hel-lo!
Or as they say in the East, *Namaste,*
& *Savati* —
the god in you
honors the god in me.
We need to talk.

REPORT FROM THE STREETS of FERGUSON & BEYOND

We know tales of trolls patrolling
bridges & byways out of town,
or of highwaymen, or stagecoach robbers, or thuggees,
all waylaying travelers, taking their money,
highjacking the strongbox, sometimes
leaving people dead lying on the ground.
Historical images abound
of thieves & cutthroats on the road.

Here & now,
the police play that role.
Things are the same, but different.

Trolls of old did not discriminate,
targeting wealth in motion
whatever its complexion.
They operated outside the law,
as enemies of the State.

Today's trolls in blue
represent the State
cruise in white patrol cars,
like a squadron of Lone Rangers riding Silver,
heroes in their own mind movie,
the Law at their command.

Unlike historical models,
they discriminate
carefully,
profiling, targeting
not the rich, but
poor people with the wrong shade of skin,
those they are charged
with protecting & serving.

Heavily armed
against the citizenry
with citations & bullets,
patrolling neighborhoods
like an occupying army,
backed by military hardware,
inclined by job stress & training
to escalate at hints of weary objection
or resistance,
to shoot to kill if panicked
by real or imagined threat,
they serve City Hall's
racist & classist biases,
& a voracious appetite for cash.

Victims who miss hearings
or can't pay through the nose
are served & protected
with arrest warrants,
do time in modern debtors prisons
for broken taillights,
illegal turns, failure to signal
and the like.
Jailed for lack of money.

Who can serve & protect the family
while in jail?
Who can go to work
while in jail?
Who can pay the bills
while in jail?

And who can do a damn thing
lying dead in a cell or in the street?

Ask Sandra Bland, Mchael Brown, Tamir Rice, Eric Garner, LaQuon
McDonald, Philandro Castile — Ask so many others, tragically &
needlessly cut down.
Ask the decades. Ask the historical record.

And so I must insist
BLACK LIVES MATTER
to those with dimes on their eyes
instead of Justice's blindfolds,
to those armed with hair trigger tempers & the Law,
to those with weapons of social disruption
on pads in their pockets,
& deadly weapons of destruction on their hips,
to governments exploiting & terrorizing
their own citizens,
and to all those who, with comfortable opinions,
deny full humanity to another,
not knowing in doing so, they deny their own:

BLACK LIVES MATTER.

And to those who mask denial
with smug self-approval
with the counter, "All lives matter,"
I say,
Too many unnecessary deaths speak loud.
Too many harassments, citations, arrests;
Too many fines, too many compound charges;
Too many days & nights in jails;
Too much stress; Too much suffering;
Too many, too many deaths—
drown out & expose that lame retort.

BLACK LIVES MATTER:
It must be printed in capital letters.
It must be shouted.

BLACK LIVES MATTER.

Don't fear it, hear it.
Embrace it.
Things must change.

FOR CHRIS BRANCH (1970-2002)

Why *jah*
do it Chris?
Why *jah*
leave
yr writing
& perform that one last rite?

We didn't know you.
Didn't know you
had it in you.
Why *jah*

knot the noose
& fit it round yr neck?
Why *jah*
take the time
to pick the tree,
the sturdy branch
bearing yr own name,
to bear what you could not,
the weight
of yr pain
& frame.

Why *jah*
do it Chris?
We thought we knew you
through yr words

their blaze & light
seemed healing,
necessary,
a controlled burn.
Transcendent rage.
Pure energy,
bright as a supernova
that reveals the heavens, &

then, less conspicuously,
consumes itself,
flaring & collapsing
into a black hole.

Ultimately,
the light of our understanding
couldn't penetrate
yr black hole, Chris.
We saw yr deep
black reflected
in yr event horizon
& mistook it for yr light.
We couldn't penetrate the darkness
in yr depths.

Clinical depression —
the posthumous verdict's in.
Inner turmoil
you saw as weakness, not illness:
wouldn't take the pills.

Demons,
black & white,
played tug of war with yr heart.

Coping with love
(for you *were* loved),
responsibilities, children,
fifteen minute fame's insatiable hungers,
a lalapalooza,
st. louis's dim derelict avenues
whipped you, drove you
to the dark woods
that sweltering July 4th weekend.

You had to have a plan.
to get the rope,
learn the hangman's knot,

pick the tree, the limb,
prepare to execute
the act
required calculation, discipline.

Some sd
you were declaring
yr final independence
Independence Day,
laptop left behind,
expressing yrself silently, indelibly,
symbolically,
in a piece of performance art:

the last, last poet, first
strange fruit
of the new millennium.

Fireworks lit the night sky
all over the city & nation.
You dangled
in the shimmering heat
three days
before discovered.

Flash to
yr handsome,
friendly countenance, yr voice's
torrential eloquence
on the Monday barroom stage.

Whitmanesque,
you contradicted yourself,
very well then,
& contained multitudes.

Another flash:
Society's cops chase the black kid
through the alley to the chain link fence

he tries to scale it—
in yr poem *Simba's Secret*—
they cut him down
in a hail of fire.

& on a fiery day, long
after the fireworks,
they cut you down, Chris,
did *jah* know the secret?
Was that a frozen smile
in the sweltering heat?

Success,
or failure?

Who can tell?
What j*ah*
think, Chris?

What *jah*
know? We didn't
know you.
Now we think
we know you better.

Mystery is all
jah tell us.
Mystery
is all
we know

Why jah?
Why jah?

Alone
in the forest,
it's as if a great tree
has fallen.
Listen!

OCCUPYING WALL STREET

You go down to the demonstration to stand against Wall Street.
You watch out for the police. Watch out for pepper spray,
tear gas, bullets.
You know your rights, keep a lawyer's number on you in case you
are arrested or abused.
You make your voice heard amidst the din of political obfuscation,
your very presence a cry of pain,
outrage, conscience — you've been cheated, ignored too long.
The few have pulled the strings too long.
The game's been rigged too long.
The politicians help mark the cards.
The media's in on the scam. Look at who owns them.
You need them,
but don't trust them. Their newspeak is not your language.
They are not your friends. Like the politicians you elect,
They are paid by the piper — but they can't avert their eyes because
you are not alone. There are hundreds, thousands, millions of you
in cities around the country, around the world,
You are massing in front of stone buildings to tear down walls, in
front of the banks, the corporations, the investment houses,
the bastions of power.
Walls behind which deals are cut,
papers prepared, signed, money exchanged.
Deals that can't be explained, money that can't be accounted for
by those with dimes on their eyes walking.
You have been invisible to them.
They have been waging the class warfare
they accuse you of. They have put you out of your home,
fired you from your job, polluted the air you breathe,
manipulating the money yours to earn,
to pay themselves lavishly
as you scrimp & scrounge.

You are here and you are not going away.
You are the iceberg to their Titanic.
You are the rising tide of a tsunami.

You are their chickens coming home to roost.
You are their worst nightmare.

You are We

United States
of consciousness.
U.S. US.

AMERICA LOVES GUNS MORE THAN CHILDREN

America loves its guns more than its children.
America hunts down its children in the streets,
mows them down in the schools, massacres them in the malls.

American loves its guns more than its children.
Keeps its gun with it at all times, at all costs.
Would rather wage war than feed poor kids.

Would rather everyone be armed than everyone be smart.
America loves its guns more than its children.
America carries its gun in the store, in the bar, in the church,

anywhere you might be make you feel safe? Are you packing?
America loves its guns more than its children.
America buries its children — doesn't tuck them in at night,

doesn't read them stories in bed. Instead,
America, lonely & stressed, sleeps with its gun under its pillow.
America dreams of its guns, & wakes up all wet.

America sells guns to crazy people,
its weapons of war to madmen militias.
Sells guns out of the trunks of its cars.

America loves its guns on tv, in the movies, on the news.
America loves its shooting range, its gun shows,
its American Sniper.
America is entertained by its guns. Driven insane by its guns.

America loves its guns more than its children.
America buys guns & cuts education funding.
America loan sharks its college students, devours them with debt —
    gives tax breaks to masters of war

America loves its guns more than its children.
America loves it guns while its infrastructure crumbles.

America loves its guns while its air & water thicken & sicken.

America protects gun owners, neglects the environment.
America says guns don't kill.
America is armed & dangerous.

America makes bigger & better guns — sends its children off to wars.
America is world's biggest arms merchant.
American guns are big business; big business are US.

America loves its guns while its jobs evaporate.
America is mowing down its children right & left
in the streets, in the schools, in the malls,

Mowing them down right here today,
mowing down their present, mowing down their future.
America loves its guns more than its children.

CORRECTIONS PLEASE

Change!

evil to live

living to loving

foul play to foreplay

sword to words

apart to a part

mindless to mindful

reject to respect

gun to fun

Change!

pollution to solution

brutality to humanity

greed to feed

sexism to exism

racism to gracism

me to we

Other to Brother

lies to wise
        (Bullshitting don't amount to mulch)

REVERSE ENGLISH

Water surrounds us.

We are in an island world.

There are no cars here.

We travel on foot or by water.

We cross bridges from street to street.

We get lost in narrow alleys, backtrack from dead ends.

Now we backtrack into the sea.

We leave Venice behind, leave hominid existence.

We are fish again.

Water surrounds us.

There are no cars here.

The sea is always moving

over its own past.

     *

Up on land, our bridge

to mammalian teeth, the savage kill,

perpetual war, the dark wood

where the soul wanders

losing its way—spirit

of the deep still with us.

watchful, unmoved, always moving.

     *

"Children plunge their heads into the world."

--Alfonso Gatto

As in, they've forgotten
more than we will ever know.
Baptism in a sea of information.
Come up crying & gasping for air.
Grasping the first hand offered
& ever grasping to hold on.
Nothing lasting. Nothing
lasts.

*

Sands at seventy
        sifting back into the sea.
                My tide running out.

*

LIFE

A cloud reflected
In a puddle dissolving
Under a hot sun.

KWANSABAS

(A form invented by Eugene B. Redmond, requires seven lines, seven words per line, each no more than seven letters except for names.)

VUDUN DANCE

Moon a force making waves, tide stirs

within you, ebbing, welling moon draws you

with its silver force into motion, poses

that open you like a door, wave

crashes, internal music, spirit enters you, you

enter spirit, moon ripples in water, your

dance is not yours; *loas* reside, preside.

KALI-MA
Kwansaba for Jayne Cortez (1934-2012)

she would name the evil, paint vivid

in words its garish ill nature, white

eerie glow of naked skulls illum'd dangling

exposed, clacked round her black throat dancing

as she sang in death's charnel ground,

her red tongue lolled, her blue song's

spittle shot fiery, sparks of healing light

BARAKA'S FIRE

for Amiri Baraka (1934-2014)

Baraka called out power, stirred up shit,

made us think. Not always pretty. Beat.

Off beat. His beat, blown up America,

under his scope, disease of racism probed

in harsh light. Blues People update, BAM !,

Black Arts voices lit by his fire

rage, engage, feel, be real & heal.

POWER OF THE WORD
for Barack Obama

O ba ma — "we are with you"

in Parsi tongue, yes we can we

say as one, black, white, every hue

takes your cue — shine bright son, Apollo's

trace, beam reason's saving grace — human hearts

connect with smarts — say O ba ma

there is no Other — teach, my brother

DOUBLE KWANSABA AFTER MICHAEL BROWN

When police are the threat, who's there
to protect? When walking in the street
can get you busted, shot, or beat
just for being black, talking back, looking
wrong, or looking strong—how can we
really be: a viable city, where people
can live in harmony? a free country?

With tanks in the street, who or
what do they defeat? No good results,
only bad; fear is what drives us
mad. And fear, the root of hate,
becomes the Police State. Instead of tear
gas, hear us! Let's relate, for a
start, human to human, heart to heart.

A FEW HAIKU

MEDITATION

Don't look back — this mo-
    ment is so full, it spills o-
      ver into the next

FOR MILES DAVIS IN 5-7-5

Miles & miles & miles
      & miles & miles & miles &
        KIND OF BLUE haiku

MY NATIONALISM

I pledge allegiance
      to the world's greatest nation —
Imagination

GOLDEN AGE

Man is estranged from that with which he is most familiar. –Charles
Olson

Man is estranged from his imagination. – Andre Breton

Can you see it, Children of Abraham.
The landscape of the mind where milk & honey flows.
Where cross, crescent, star make one universe, one
Omni-directional firmament spinning in harmony
Like wheels of sun, moon, galaxies, time – i.e. the Divine Plan.

Can you hear it, Children of Abraham,
Listening to the voice within, like Rumi, Jesus, Abulafia.
Listening like Nanak
To your own silent voice welling up.
Can you hear it?

Can you feel it, yourself expanding as you open.
The warmth filling you, call it love.
Compassion.
The getting from giving.

Can you re-focus, adjust your vision, Children of Abraham.
Can you turn on the light.
Can you imagine the riches of harmony.
Can you count the blessings, tabulate the wealth of peace.
And imagine, it all
Adds up
to One.

Can you see it.
A thousand years ago in Spain, Christian, Jewish, Muslim
Poets, philosophers, musicians opening the door
To a Golden Age. Can you see it
can be, has been, must be done.

The time is now, Children of Abraham.
You have suffered so much, caused so much suffering
Rattling mind forged manacles
The throbbing heart can shatter.

You have known so much, Children of Abraham.
You know so much,
But can you see, can you hear,
Can you imagine, can you feel?

HASDAI IBN SHAPRUT

1.

"Prince of the Jews,"
in Cordoba, at the end of the first millennium,
knew the antidotes for poisons--
Doctor Hasdai
found himself
in demand
by the royal & ruling families.

Who was this Jew with clout who
translated the pharmacology,
saw deeply into human nature,
wrote poems,
practiced healing arts &
embarked on diplomatic missions
to Baghdad & Bergundy,
to Otto Uno of Germany
for Abdl al-Rachmann?

Hasdai!
A Jew with personality,
a healer, a man of knowledge,
a talker, a guy
who could converse with anyone,
anywhere, highborn or low,
existing or even, maybe no--
Hasdai, projected
imagination into space,
the Prince of the Jews
wrote to Joseph, King of the legendary Khazars,
somewhere out there
beyond the Empire's boundaries.
Did His Majesty really exist? he inquired.
What was his tribe? His Judaism like?
Did he know when the Messiah was coming?
His arrival seemed long overdue.

"O Blessed is the Lord of Israel," intoned Hasdai,
from Spain, to his desire, "who has not left us
without an independent kingdom. . . ."

Hasdai, centered, but on the margin — emissary,
laison, connection, great tree
rooted deep in Spanish soil, but branching out,
embracing other branches, shading
as it reaches for the heavens, spreading
the dream
the dream of Hasdai — dream of a Jew, dream
splattered & streaming
in all directions, portable dream, bearing the home
inside
the dream,
the central fire,
burning bush,
glow of ember letters, kindling,
energizing the survival, shaping
words, poems, illuminating
the suffering--
the burning Temples, charred scrolls,
acrid cinders, powdery bones,
the headaches, the glow
between the brows, the dream
of life. Transcending.
Transforming. Hasdai

the healer repairs damage,
founds schools for Jewish children,
spends his wealth buying old manuscripts
so that the Word would never be lost,
protests directly to the Bishops of Burgos
their Easter-time ritual humiliations of the Jews: God,
he reminds them, sees everything,
& never forgets; Hasdai,
the right hand man,
gathers a courtyard full of poets & philosophers

a chorus of Muslims, Christians, & Jews
to please His Majesty.

Shapes the dream
of a golden age,
the idea of
a beautiful garden
in Spain's courtyard, one
filled with intermingling fragrances,
harmonic voices,
multi-colored flowers of every description,
a garden not in some distant land,
some distant, mythical past,
a garden here & now in Sepharad;

Hasdai planting, nurturing,
the dream seeds of Hasdai,
a cosmopolitan Jew,
a Jew who knew
the antidotes for poisons,
the sweetness of the tongue, the sharing
of the soul-stuff,
a healer,
a Jew who delivered
the royal birth.
Hasdai stoops,
gathering sparks
to light the way.

2.

A thousand years later,
at the end of the second millennium,
I write your name, Hasdai,
I write 'Sepharad', opening its gates of mind,
living a kind of dream
that might have been yours,
beaming on my screen in letters of light,
projecting clusters of sparkling

singers, bards of every complexion.
A courtyard, a cafe, a dark bar, a magazine.
A living room.
Is this what it is to be poet?
a unified effort
cutting through time?
a ceremony of mending & healing?
a language so precise
it blurs all boundaries?
the more you are yourself,
the more you are not?
one mind?
a march of names?
shards of light?

Sepharad gleams at the end of the highway.

A MAN OF LETTERS
for Abraham Abulafia (1240-1291)

I. THE ART OF SKIPPING

I invoke the holy spirit.
I chant the words of Creation.
I blend the letters.
I write the holy books.
I name their names. Yes.
I scribe *The Life of the Soul.*
I uncover *The Mysteries of the Torah.*
I write *The Book of Redemption.*
I reveal *The Life of the Future World.*
I record *The Book of Testimonies.*
From me, *The Book of the Covenant.*
I disclose *The Book of the Human Man.*
I open *The Light of the Intellect.*
I make *The Book of the Sign.*
I turn *The Key of Wisdoms.*
I inscribe *The Words of Beauty.*
I create *The Book of Passion.*
I teach *The Book of Blendings.*

◆

My name is Abulafia. I am divine.
I carry many names.
I was born in Saragosa, in the kingdom of Spain.
You can call me Abraham. Zachariah. Raziel.
I will call you by your name.
I chant the names of God.
I ride each flaming letter.
I burn with light & love.
I am Abulafia: Abraham, Zachariah, Raziel.

My teachers taught me
the word's power:

My teachers were my father,
my nature,
Maimonides,
& Rabbi Hillel.

◆

When my father died, I was eighteen.
I began my wanderings.
I traveled over land & sea
to the Holy Land, seeking the river Sambation.
dreaming of finding Israel's lost tribes.
In the year 5019 I reached Acco, in Egypt,
where Maimonides had lived.
I could feel his spirit.

Ishmael & Esau were waging war
all around us, & I could go no further.
I heard Maimonides' voice whisper in a breeze,
the tribes are forever scattered
& you too must leave — imagination,
thought, prophecy, words, letters:
these are your journey's paths.

I shifted directions — over deserts,
to India, up mountains to Tibet vast wanderings
through heavenly landscapes,
mountainous realms of mind,.
I met many radiant guides.

I left my body many times.
I returned aglow, like Moses descending,
like the Ark of the Covenant
beneath its pure white cloth.

I always returned, to time, to space,
to the familiar world of days.
I travelled back
through Ottoman's lands,

married in Salonika, practiced & wrote,
till the writing became the practice
& the practice the proof.

A few disciples came to me
& called me Rabbi;
I showed them what I knew.

My method was thus:
I meditated on the letters —
for from the word came the creation,
& from the letters came the word.
I tallied each word's numbers — their sums & correspondences.
I maneuvered & blended the letters & explored their power
in their new combinations, through chanting & through thought.

Because behind the letters was something else:
an intention.
And beyond intention was something else:
a desire.
And beyond desire was something else:
a feeling.
And beyond feeling was something else:
a stirring.
And beyond the stirring was something else
still.

Out of the stillness, I chanted their sounds,
chanted the seventy-two permutations
of the name of God, arranged the flaming letters
in great symmetric spirals
& feasted my eyes till I
was no longer there; I flew away
& became what I beheld.

When I was thirty-one, in Barcelona, God awakened me
from my sleep, & I learned the *Sefer Yetsirah*
with its commentaries. God's hand was upon me,
& I wrote books of wisdom & wondrous prophecy.

My soul awakened within me,
& the spirit of God touched my mouth.
An experience of holiness fluttered through me,
& I saw many fearsome sights & wonders,
through signs & miracles.

◆

I described how
I set myself the task at night
of combining letters with one another
& of pondering over them,
chanting them,
in philosophical meditation.
You guide your thinking step by step
first by means of script & language
& then by means of mind & imagination.
You skip, a marvelous means of mental athletics —
& by skipping move further & further out beyond the boundaries.
I would let the consonants fly
through the air rapidly
& the room would become warm
& the warmth would rise
inside me. The combinations of letters become
beyond familiarity & meaning,
beyond the limits the mind has set for them.

The third night
I nodded off a little,
quill in hand,
& paper on my knees.
Then I noticed the candle
was about to go out.
I watched its weak flame waver, dim,
&, as I rose to try to right it,
the flame died.

The flame was out.
But the light continued.

I was greatly astonished.
Was I dreaming?
Then I realized
that the light radiated
from me.

"I don't believe it!" I exclaimed.
I walked to & fro
throughout the house, &
behold! the light remained with me
all the while.
I lay on a couch & covered myself up &
behold! the light was
still with me!
I could see my hand before my face
under the cover.

I said
this is truly a great sign
& a new phenomenon.
I have been blessed.

◆

During the second week
the power of meditation
became so strong in me
that, as I sat breathing rhythmically
before my book, I could not write down the letters
that spurted of their own volition from my pen.
The page was a mess of blotches.
Had there been ten people present
they could not write down
all the many combinations that came to me
during the influx.

◆

I stopped.
& at midnight,
when the power especially gains strength,
& the body weakens,
I began again.
I set out
to chant the Great Name of God,
consisting of seventy-two names —
I combined, permuted, & chanted
the sacred sounds of the letters.

Every letter is a whole world.
A body of light floating in the universe.
The world of each letter is a world of bliss.

I followed the path
of the names —
the more
I chanted, the more
they became pure sound —
& the less understandable the name
the higher the order of revelation & experience —
I abstracted words from thought
following wherever they led
until I passed beyond
the territory of the natural mind —
chanting the 72 names of God
until the letters took on in my eyes the shapes of mountains —
I did not stop but climbed
until I arrived at last
not at a place but at an energy —
I was within the activity of a force
beyond my control.
Strong trembling seized me.
I could summon no strength —
my hair stood on end.
And behold! something resembling speech
emerged from my heart
& came to my lips, forcing them to move.

I thought—God forbid!—perhaps this
is the spirit of madness that has entered into me.
I shouted, Why do you make me struggle!
I only seek God out of love & need.

Oil fell on me, as on one anointed
& the speech began again, & behold—
I heard it uttering wisdom.

◆

You must rest.

But if you get this far
you must go on.

You must try another exercise,
designed to draw thought forth
slowly, deeply,
from its source:

As you breathe the way I show you,
the mind will quicken
& finally flood
with a torrent of images, words, letters
spinning vividly & each demanding utterance
while eluding grasp—
until the force is so intense
that you cannot speak.

This is but a stage.
You can still go further, riding the power
through the imagination,
till the force takes the form
of a polished mirror.

You go a little further,
entering this mirror
like going through a doorway,

& you realize
that your inmost being
lies outside.

II. THE DARK SIDE OF THE WHITE SEEDS

"And God said to Zachariah, the healthy one,
'Go, & I will send you to the people who are stricken in heart,
to heal their sickness. Take with you the remedy of My Name . . .'
And God gave a gift of grace & a portion of love to Zachariah,
& he went about in the lands of the nations where Israel was scattered."

But the spirits of jealousy gathered round me.

"Those who would deny the highest wisdom stood up,
sick & stricken with deadly wounds."

The Rashba called me a fraud and a disgusting creature.
Rabbi Chayit called me mad, & actually claimed
that since the destruction of the second temple
"prophecy has been given over to the insane."
Rabbi Yashar called me worse than worthless.

"The hearts of those who followed melted,
& their spirit became weak,
& they stopped following those who knew the Name."

But the Chayid met me & told the people I was a great rabbi,
& so I persevered, rising and falling, buffeted by waves
& winds from within & without.

Like Zachariah
my name was scorned.

I offered the healing power of God's name & remembrance & love
but only a few of the sages of Israel opened their ears & hearts,
& none of the sickest were among them.

"& God awakened the spirit of Zachariah
to review & double his prophetic books . . .
& it was in those days that God said to Zachariah,
"Write for you this book, that will go against the sages of Israel
in this generation, who boast about that which I do not desire.
They say, Why should we consider God's Name,
how will it benefit us if we utter it,
& how will it benefit us if we calculate it? . . .
So they chased him from city to city, & place to place. . ."

I began writing my books.
I had four desciples in Capua, and four in Agripoli —
none were worthy. I witheld from them the Truth.
In Rome, there were two old men, Rabbi Tazdikia
& Rabbi Yeshiah. I had some success with them,
but they were very old, & they died.
I taught Rabbi Kolynymos of blessed memory
in Barcelona, & Rabbi Solomon, a single man
& one of the leaders of the community,
a brilliant student.
In Burgos I taught Rabbi Moshe Sifno, a master,
& his desciple, Rabbi Shem Tov, a sweet young man,
but too young. I could only scratch the surface with them.
In Medina Celi I had two desciples: Samuel the Prophet
& Joseph Gikatila; both learned the light of Kaballah.

My method was my madness.
I rode higher & further out,
& crashed down lower & deeper down
& couldn't rise.

I was criticized in the Temples.
I was slandered in the streets.
I, Raziel, was confronted with fantasy & error, driven mad by
what my eyes saw. At times my mind was totally confused.

I could not find anyone else like me,
who could teach me the correct path.
For fifteen years, Satan was at my right hand
to mislead me. My study became a sepulcher. . .
I murdered with my white seed.

I killed. I lied. I cheated. I stole.
I was & am unworthy. What am I, but a man.
I breathe in only to breathe out.
I rise only to fall.
My words dropped heavily like dark shells.

& then in the ninth year of my prophecy, I flew off,
like a lost angel
imbued with a spirit of certainty.
If no one would listen I would insist.

"And God commanded him to speak in His Name to the gentiles,
uncircumcised in heart, & uncircumcised in flesh. . ."

A voice came in the night, & told me to convert the Pope.

I stood on a box in the street outside the Temple in Barcelona
& announced my intent. Then I set off for Rome.
I got as far as Tarni, where the Jews denounced me,
& the Christians threw me in jail.
But a miracle occurred, & Raziel escaped.
I settled a year in Capua
to lick my wounds & write *The Book of Life.*

Then the voice said, Raziel, you must go.
I approached Rome in time to meet with the Pope
on the day before Rosh Ha Shonah.
But he had heard of my journey
& had gone off to Saronno, a day's trip away,
leaving word with his gatekeepers
that if Raziel should come to speak to him in the name of Judaism,
I should be detained, taken out
& burned at the stake. He had left the wood prepared

just inside the gates of the city.

I paused upon hearing this. I prayed & meditated
& saw great wonders which I wrote down
in *The Book of Testimonies*.

On the day I was to see the Pope
I was given two mouths.
One spoke words of this world, one of another.
The light was strange as I passed through the gates.
A messenger greeted me as I entered
& told me that he who would have me killed,
the Pope I had journeyed to see,
had died himself, unexpectedly,
the night before, apparently of the plague.

One was killed that night, & one was saved.
I praise God, his miracles, his mysterious ways.

The Little Brothers then imprisoned me:
they locked me in their academy for one moon's span
then set me free.

I prayed to God & the power filled me,
surging like a lover's bliss for his beloved.
Mouth to mouth I — Abulafia, Abraham, Zachariah, Raziel —
spoke to Him, uttering all His names
in a transporting kiss.
I embraced, I entered, I was subsumed.
Gladness settled on my soul & trembling filled my body,
I was like one who rides rapidly on a horse
who is happy & joyful,
while the horse trembles beneath him.

I cried out, & crashed back into my self.
I held my ecstasy in my hand, limp & deflated.
I despised myself, who had presumed to speak.

I murdered with my white seed.

All I saw for months were
glowing beings, instances as long as a blink,
fireflies flicking out in the space before my eyes
where sacred letters once had flamed.
Stains of shame stuck to the page.

But God had been with me from the year one, & finally
gave me counsel.
God had mercy upon me, though I was weak.
God helped me to stand my ground
though I was set upon from all sides.
God helped me withstand the tests, the delusions,
the darkness, & enlightened my heart.

I, Abulafia —
Abraham, Zachariah, Raziel.
My names are masks.

Whoever is full of himself has no room for God.

HOMAGE TO TEN IN TEN LINES

1. I stood on ten toes
2. I prayed with ten fingers
3. I witnessed the ten plagues devour Egypt
4. I descended from the ten lost tribes
5. I bowed before the ten commandments
6. I opened the Torah's ark as part of a minion
7. I walked in the creation uttered by ten powerful
                        words
8. I wandered in a universe structured by the ten
sephiroth, the divine program
9. String theory & Mahayana Buddhists placed me in
the ten dimensions
10. I collaborated with the nine muses to write
my poems

EXILE

    for Judah Halevi (1075-1141)

O Jerusalem! O Sepharad!
O mortal exile, eternal longing!
You, Jerusalem, embody all in your towers —
home to my spirit, Sabbath Bride, Shekina,
God — with your *signs to Jacob's seed*
that they shall ever be a nation.
Farewell Toledo. (Holy Toledo!)
Good-bye Granada & all my medicinal healings.

My heart is in the East
  and I am at the edge of the West.

Beyond the body now.
I am bound to heal the soul.

Overland, then by ship through turbulent seas,
the trial begins. And overland again:

Time has tossed me toward Egypt's deserts,
  but tell it to hurl me further
    until I see the desert of Judah.

Endless footprints in the endless sands.
Alexandria, Damietta, Fustaf near Cairo, then the caravans —
O desert, parch my thirst, test me further.
Blazing heat, sandstorms, lost bearings.
In Tyre, I am haggard, & white haired.
In Damascus I am wild eyed & despairing of
ever reaching Jerusalem.
& yet I go on.

               ◆

Did Judah Ha-Levi make it to Jeruasalem?
Did he find God? Or God find him?
Or did he die an obscure and anonymous death

never achieving his goal?

There is no evidence Halevi ever made it to Jerusalem.

But a legend persists
that he did reach the hillside overlooking the city.
There he paused, overcome
by finally seeing the beautiful towers
of the ancestral home that had obsessed
and meant so much to him.
He burst out in song, his most beautiful elegy, "Zionides."

Then a thief leaped out of the shadows,
attacked him, stabbed him & left him for dead.

He had been robbed of his life & his goal.
Or had he been fulfilled?

In my going out to meet you
I found you coming toward me.

RAGE

for Solomon Ibn Gabirol (1021-1057)

He longs to give form to the formless
as a man longs for his friend

the worst is the coldness
between you & me,
the heart contracts,
blood spurts & pocks at the skin,
red pustules erupt, offend
the world, the universe,
the heart of God,
you — it is all formless —
the room is cold
as Ha-Nagid's poems —
& I, a poet, am longing
for form, a fountain say,
a source of light welling up inside —
call it's warmth love,
call its purity God —

I write on,
a ravished human,
the pus of life
my reward
sometimes a flash
illuminates
the dim fog,
a poem coalesces
out of nothing
a oneness
a residue
of your glance

I am living
dying

alone-
what is worst is the coldness
the empty space
between the stars

100 THOUSAND POETS FOR CHANGE
for Michael Rothenberg & Terri Carrion, Sept. 24, 2011

Poets blowing
in the winds of change
blowing truth to open ears
blowing truth in the face of fears

whispering wind
howling wind
Poets blowing
round the world

blowing light
& blowing rain
renewing life
& easing pain

Poets blowing
everywhere
scattering seeds
against despair

Poets blowing
the human spirit
Poets blowing
can you hear it?

Can you hear it
corporations?
Can you hear it
sold out nations?

Change is blowing
because it must
Change is blowing
because it's just

Poets blowing
in a worldwide choir.
Poets blowing
to inspire

Change is what
our planet needs
Poems are seeds
That lead to deeds.

RE: BIRTHDAY ST. LOUIS TWO FIFTY

Mississippians lived here, Cahokians
built largest city north of Tenochitlan's;
traded with peoples of the Great Lakes, Rocky Mounts,
Atlantic Coast, Mexico & more;
left mysterious mounds & powerful spirit
in the earth around our shore.

Osage, Ponca, Omaha, Kawpaw & Paw
all came, moved in, moved on, often in tears.
Native Americans here, by the banks of the great river,
Great Spirit, a thousand years.

250 years since most recent humans gathered, new as
Neo-Mississippians — that is, St. Louis.
Trappers & traders remade us as a center,
& re-opened the gateway for others to enter.
Peoples descended from river folk —
Congo, Yangtse, Loire, Rhine, Tigris & Indus —
great human rivers pouring & trickling into St. Louis —
from every land, from every nation,
from mountains, deserts, prairie & plain,
some supplied & moved on, while many remained,
sensing a spirit by the great river's shore,
a power spot, a place to stay, & be re-born.
Europeans, Africans, Asians, Americans all
responding to the river's call.

St. Louis, Mound City, River City,
city of baseball, blues, & beer,
an iconic American city established here.

Still a youngster on the millennial scale,
new when measured on the Mississippian timeline.
Will our best days lie ahead as we enter our prime?

I too was reborn here — picked up on the spirit in the air,

at a time when people made statements with their hair;
Creeley, Ginsberg, Redmond, LeFlore
opened up wide my poetry door.
Snyder administered the boddhisatva vow
to use words to bring light to the eternal now —
where everyone suffers, as the great Buddha teaches,
& love is the answer, as sweet Jesus preaches.

We live by the heartbeat.

The great river, North America's pulse,
throbs in us, in our bustling businesses, our blood, our spirit,
flows into our music that animates the world.

The river's timeless depths inform & challenge.
Its dynamic oneness models our future.

In the past our daughters & sons
have pioneered new directions.

Mr. Handy, Miles Davis, Chuck Berry, Scott Joplin,
opened the world's ears to musical innovation
infused with the river's vital vibration.

T.S. Eliot, Tennessee Williams, William Burroughs,
Kate Chopin & Maya Angelou,
travelled with the river's spirit, liberating writing
with fresh language & points of view.

Henry Shaw & Barry Commoner
picked up on the current from the depths of the river
& embraced nature's healing & energy potential
seeding a healthy future that now is essential.

Masters & Johnson stripped our denial bare,
laid us naked as the river
to make us more self accepting, self aware.

Our smarts & arts have represented us well.

Soul baring writers!
Music for the world to move to, groove to!
Oneness with nature within us & without!
Consciousness expansion! healing power! solar solutions!
Keys to our troubled world's survival, & to ours,
begins with us.

And the next two fifty begins a story
that can lead to disaster or to glory.
Will we be happy in our city's mature years?
Will we get beyond our lingering, limiting fears?
For fear is at the root of hate,
a poison to individual & collective fate.

And we have certain obligations
to current & future generations.

Can we invest minds & money with wisdom & sanity
to support what's best for our common humanity?

Can we provide *all* kids good education
so some won't be mired in stagnation
& instead can rise above their station
& add their great gifts to a great nation?

It's time for this & other conversations.

Will we be known as a city of the gun,
or as one that nurtures life like the sun?

Will we leave as testament
a clean pristine environment?

& can we relate to the Other
as a sister or a brother,
as children of God & the great Earth Mother?

Black, white, yellow, red —
What matters is what's in your heart & head.

Homophobia, racism, sexism —
These all need to be ex-isms.

What we need is to talk; we're all human beings,
together we can accomplish great things.

Soul to soul, & heart to heart
is the best & only place to start.

As in the East they say *Namaste* and *Savati* —
the god in you honors the god in me.

And as mystics reveal throughout history
the paradoxical universal mystery's key
is unity within diversity.

I declare this ST. LOUIS'S RE-BIRTH-DAY!
A time to heal, drive fear away.

The first two fifty we've made our mark
with our smarts & with our arts.
The future already marks our deeds,
hums to our beat, will sow our seeds

The next two fifty, more smarts, more arts,
& a focus on our hearts.

Time for St. Lou Is, truly, to become
St. Lou Us. All of us — one polity
with mutual R-E-S-P-E-C-T,
a unity community,
less of me & more of we
to harness the energy of our DIVERCity;

When each part is great, the whole is greater.
Let St. Louis be the incubator.
Our sameness and our variety, united, creates synergy.
Open heart, open mind, fulfill the ends of human*kind*.

One with nature, one with each other,
we fulfill ourselves, what we are here for
Fully human, free of stress, each a distinct wave
in the river's dynamic oneness.

And each wave is a living river,
a river flowing toward an infinite sea,
all of our ultimate destiny.

But now, our finite stay on earth,
is when we have to prove our worth.

Let us be reborn, renewed, & move forward this re-birth day,
& let our smarts, arts & hearts lead US on our way.

This poem written to fulfill a requirement of St. Louis's first Poet Laureate, to write a poem relating to the 250th anniversary of the city in 2014.

About the Poet

Michael Castro, called "a legend in St. Louis poetry" by Charles Guenther in the *St. Louis Post Dispatch*, is a widely published poet and translator. Castro is a founder of the literary organization and magazine *River Styx*, in continuous operation since 1975. He has spread the word of poetry off the page for decades, organizing readings and hosting three literary radio programs. He has read his poems on four continents, including many collaborative performances with musicians. His aural/oral work is recorded on seven albums. With his fellow poet Gabor G. Gyukics he has translated modern Hungarian poetry, resulting in five books. Castro is the recipient of the Guardian Angel of St. Louis Poetry Award from River Styx, the Warrior Poet Award from Word in Motion, and the Traditions of Literary Excellence Award from the St. Louis Literary Consortium all for lifetime achievement. In 2015 he was named St. Louis's first Poet Laureate.

WORKS BY MICHAEL CASTRO

POETRY

Ripple (with Michael Corr, Alan Fleck, & Jay Zelenka), poems & woodcuts, Hard Times Press, 1970.

The Kokopilau Cycle, Blue Cloud Quarterly Press, 1975, long poem.

Ghost Highways & Other Homes, Cornerstone Press, 1976, poems.

Cracks, The Cauldron Press, 1977, poems.

(US), Ridgeway Press, 1991, poems.

River City Rhapsody, (with Eugene B. Redmond, Jane Bidleman, and Marcia Cann, *Drum Voices Revue* Special Editionpoem for the inauguration of Freeman Bosley Jr. as St. Louis's first African-American Mayor), 1993.

The Man Who Looked Into Coltrane's Horn, Caliban Press, 1997, long poem.

Human Rites, Neshui Press, 2000, poems.

The Bush Years, JK Publishing, 2010, poems.

The Guide: Maimonides' Journey, Shulamis Press, 2014, long poem.

How Things Stack Up, Singing Bone Press, 2014, poems.

PROSE

Interpreting the Indian: Twentieth Century Poets and the Native American, University of New Mexico Press, 1984; paperback edition, University of Oklahoma Press, 1991.

TRANSLATIONS (with Gabor G. Gyukics)

Swimming in the Ground: Contemporary Hungarian Poetry, Neshui Press, 2001.

Gypsy Drill: Poems of Attila Balogh, Hungarian edition, Neshui Press, 2005.

A Transparent Lion: Selected Poetry of Attila Jozsef, Green Integer Books, 2006.

Terrenum (The Place of Time), poetry and art by Adam Gall, Hungarian edition, Budapest, Eletrajz Kalliatasok Publications, 2010.

My God, How Many Mistakes I've Made: The Poetry of Endre Kukorelly, (Singing Bone Press, 2015

RECORDINGS

Scenes from the Gateway, with Exiles: Jay Zelenka and Gregory Mills (Esfoma Recordings, 1987).

Freedom Ring: with the Fred Tompkins Poetry &
Music Ensemble: (tompkinsjazz.com 2001).

Curve Extended, with the Fred Tomkins Poetry &
Music Ensemble (tompkinsjazz.com 2004).

Deep Mirror with Joe Catalano (Freedonia Music
2008).

Kokopilau with J.D. Parran (Freedonia Music
2008).

Needle of Light with James Marshall's Human
Arts Ensemble (Freedonia Music, 2011).

*STL Free Jazz Collective: Live at the Sheldon Concert
Hall* (2016)

COLLECTIONS

*Trumpet in the Morning: Poems of Arthur Brown
(1985)*

The Best of River Styx (1995))

*Crossing the Divide: St Louis Poets on Social Issues
(2016)*

Acknowledgements: The author would like to thank the editors of the following anthologies, magazines, e-zines, and newspapers who have published poems collected here:

Periodicals

Abaxas, Art Today, Auration, B-Zine, Bezoar, Big Bridge, Break Bread With the World, Brilliant Corners, Bulletin of the Missouri Philological Society, Contact II Postcard Series, The Cumberland Review, Edge (Japan), , Fat Chance, Fireweed, The Forest Park Review, The Greenfield Review, Grist, , Ignite, Intermission, International Poetry (Brazil), Image, Isthmus, , Literati Chicago, Long Shot, KWMU Blog, , The Midwest Quarterly, Milk, Miscellany (India), The Mississippi Valley Review, Natural Bridge, Nexus, Noctiluca, The North Country Almanac, Pathfinder, Poems for Your Pocket, Observable Readings 2006-2007, The Pittsburgh Quarterly, Printed Matter, River Styx, Shuffle Boil, The St. Louis American, , St. Louis Magazine, The St. Louis Post-Dispatch, STL Today, The Tampa Review, Telephone, Truck, Untamed Ink, Velocity, Visions, Visions International, World Poetry, Woven Tales

Anthologies

And What Rough Beast: Poems at the End of the Century, The Bloomsbury Anthology of Jewish American Poetry, , The Border Crossed Us, First Harvest: Jewish American Writing in St. Louis, Flood Stage: an Anthology of Writing in St. Louis, Focus Midwest, Half Naked Muse (Hungary), How to Eat a Poem, Imagining the Jewish God, Life, Liberty, and the Pursuit of Poetry, Memories and Memoirs: Essays, Poems, Stories and Letters by Missouri Authors, The Nuke Chronicles, Rise, Rising Waters: Reflections on the Year of the Great Flood, Roof, The Sagarin Review, The Second Set: The Jazz Anthology, Sparks of Fire: Blake in a New World Age, St. Louis Noir, Voices from the Interior: The Missouri Poets, Winter Harvest: Jewish Writing in St. Louis 2006-2011, World Edge (Japan),

www.ingramcontent.com/pod-product-compliance
Lightning Source LLC
LaVergne TN
LVHW051452080426
835509LV00017B/1749